Human Factors and Aerospace Safety
AN INTERNATIONAL JOURNAL

Volume 1, Number 1	2001

Preface

A new international journal in aviation safety   1
Don Harris and Helen C. Muir

Position Paper

Reviewing the role of cockpit alerting systems   5
Amy R. Pritchett

Formal Papers

The disembodiment of data in the analysis of human factors accidents   39
Sidney W. A. Dekker

Applying Reason: the human factors analysis and classification system (HFACS)   59
Scott A. Shappell and Douglas A. Wiegmann

Quantity and quality of sleep during the record manned space flight of 438 days   87
Alex Gundel, Jürgen Drescher and Valeri V. Polyakov

Critical Incidents

Precautionary emergency evacuations: is it better to be safe *and* sorry?   99
Lauren Thomas

Calendar of Events   102

First published 2001 by Ashgate Publishing

Reissued 2018 by Routledge
2 Park Square, Milton Park, Abingdon, Oxon OX14 4RN
711 Third Avenue, New York, NY 10017, USA

Routledge is an imprint of the Taylor & Francis Group, an informa business

Published quarterly © 2001 Taylor & Francis

If you are in the USA, you may photocopy portions of this Journal only for personal use. For libraries and others registered, copying is governed by the US Copyright Law Sections 107 and 108, and requires a fee paid to Copyright Clearance Centre Inc., 21 Congress St., Salem, MA 01970, detailing the Journal name and its ISSN, Volume, Number and pages concerned. Any other copying is prohibited without the publishers' consent in writing.

All rights reserved. No part of this book may be reprinted or reproduced or utilised in any form or by any electronic, mechanical, or other means, now known or hereafter invented, including photocopying and recording, or in any information storage or retrieval system, without permission in writing from the publishers.

Notice:
Product or corporate names may be trademarks or registered trademarks, and are used only for identification and explanation without intent to infringe.

Publisher's Note
The publisher has gone to great lengths to ensure the quality of this reprint but points out that some imperfections in the original copies may be apparent.

Disclaimer
The publisher has made every effort to trace copyright holders and welcomes correspondence from those they have been unable to contact.

A Library of Congress record exists under LC control number: 2005008921

ISBN 13: 978-1-138-63632-3 (hbk)
ISBN 13: 978-1-138-63633-0 (pbk)
ISBN 13: 978-1-315-20394-2 (ebk)

ISSN 1468 9456

PREFACE

A new international journal in aviation safety

Don Harris and Helen C. Muir
Editors-in-Chief
Cranfield University, UK

Why a new journal?

The last half of the 20th Century saw a steady year-on-year growth in air transport, typically in the region of 5% per year during the 1990s. The first year of the 21st Century shows no evidence for any slow down in this rate of expansion. Unfortunately, the increase in air traffic has not been accompanied by a corresponding decrease in the accident rate. During the last ten years, for North American and Western European built aircraft, this has remained relatively static at approximately one hull loss accident per million departures. It is envisaged that the number of aircraft in service world-wide will double by the year 2015, to approximately 23,000 aircraft. If there is no significant improvement in the accident rate from the current figure, this will mean one major hull-loss accident every week (Graeber and Mumaw, 1999).

There have been significant advances in the engineering design and production standards of the hardware and electronics in commercial aircraft in the corresponding period. It is now uncommon for the principal (or sole) cause of an aircraft accident to be a component failure. Human error is now implicated in up to 80% of all civil and military aviation accidents, (see Shappell and Wiegmann, this volume). The human being is now arguably the least reliable component left in the system. This basic premise forms the basis for this new international journal, *Human Factors and Aerospace Safety*. The Journal focuses specifically on the human element in the aerospace system (civil or military) and its role in either causing accidents or incidents, or in promoting safety. The journal solicits

Correspondence: Don Harris or Helen C. Muir, Human Factors Group, College of Aeronautics, Cranfield University, Cranfield, Bedford, MK43 0AL, UK; or d.harris/h.muir@cranfield.ac.uk contributions from both academic researchers and practitioners from industry. Human factors and safety are applied sciences and this will be reflected in the tone and composition of papers in the journal.

In the current context, human factors encompasses the study of psychology, ergonomics, human engineering and human physiology/medicine with the objective of improving safety, through the optimisation of the human element in the system or by improving the human-machine interface. *Human Factors and Aviation Safety* encourages submissions from practitioners and researchers in all these disciplines.

Although the ultimate objective in the aviation industry is to reduce the accident rate it would be wrong to focus solely on the aircraft and its flight crew to achieve this aim. The aviation safety system extends far beyond this. No aircraft can operate safely without significant efforts from design engineers, maintenance engineers, air traffic controllers, airport security operatives and the regulator, to name but a few. It would also be incorrect to assume that safety is all about primary safety measures (i.e. those aimed at stopping the accident from happening). Secondary safety (ameliorating the consequences of the accident once it has happened) is also important.

In 1957 with the launch of Sputnik, the aviation industry became the aerospace industry. The 1990s saw the increasing exploitation of space for scientific, military and commercial purposes. The manned and unmanned exploitation continues to increase, but just because a spaceflight may be unmanned does not mean to say that there are no human factors considerations in ensuring its safety. Safety in spaceflight is critical, perhaps even more so than operations within the Earth's atmosphere. The opportunities for recovery are considerably more complex and limited. The increase in out-of-atmosphere flight is reflected in the title of the Journal.

Composition of the Journal

Three broad categories of scientific paper appear in *Human Factors and Aviation Safety*:
- **Research papers** describing new research into the area of human factors and aviation safety.
- **Practitioner papers** describing successful safety initiatives or case studies (for example accident case studies)
- **Position papers** providing a critical overview of a particular area of human factors and aviation safety with the aim of developing theory and setting a research agenda for the future.

In every issue there will be one final short section, **Critical Incidents**, taking a look at human factors issues appearing in accident and incident databases from around the world. The object of this section is to draw the attention of practitioners and researchers to emerging safety issues.

In addition to these papers a Calendar of events will appear in every issue keeping the readership informed of forthcoming world-wide events concerned with human factors and aerospace safety. From time-to-time book reviews of selected volumes will also be published.

On behalf of the Associate Editors and all the Members of the Editorial Board we would like to take this opportunity to welcome you to the Journal. We hope that you will find its content interesting, stimulating and useful.

Don Harris and Helen C. Muir

Cranfield University
October 2000

References

Graeber, R.C. and Mumar, R. J. (1999). Realising the benefits of cognitive engineering in commercial aviation. In, D. Harris (Ed), *Engineering Psychology and Cognitive Ergonomics - Volume Three* (pp. 3-26). Aldershot: Ashgate.

Shappell, S.A. and Wiegmann, D.A. (2001). Applying Reason: the human factors analysis and classification system (HFACS). *Human Factors and Aerospace Safety, 1,* 59-86.

POSITION PAPER

Reviewing the role of cockpit alerting systems

Amy R. Pritchett
Georgia Institute of Technology, USA

Abstract

Alerting systems are a prevalent part of modern cockpits, involved in a wide range of piloting tasks. This increasing prevalence corresponds with the increasing capability of modern alerting systems, which have sophisticated, complex algorithms referencing many input sources. The role(s) of the cockpit alerting system have expanded beyond the attention-director role normally covered in the research literature, including nuisances, desired cues, overloads, task management aids, initiators of procedures, and command devices. Some of these roles may be unintended by the designer, be problematic in terms of operational safety, or obstruct the pilot from having cognitive involvement in resolving hazards. These roles imply several problems which highlight operational issues and reveal open research topics. Some of these problems can be solved through widely-recognised measures, such as the reduction of false alarms. Other problems may be more difficult to solve; framed in automation terms, alerting systems are inherently clumsy with an opaque interface into their functioning. The most authoritative alerting systems are also prone to under- and over-reliance, and to conflicts between the authority and responsibility of the pilot. The safety benefits of alerting systems have been widely noted; however, without consideration of these human factors issues there may be a limit to further improvements in safety achievable by the addition of more alerting systems.

Correspondence: Amy R. Pritchett, 765 Ferst Drive, School of Industrial and Systems Engineering, Georgia Tech, Atlanta GA, USA 30332-0205 or amy.pritchett@isye.gatech.edu

Introduction

Alerting systems are prevalent in modern cockpits. A Boeing 777, for example, may have an Engine Indication and Crew Alerting System (EICAS) dedicated to generating alerts and status messages about on-board systems, embedded alerting within other on-board systems, stall warnings, and advanced safety systems such as windshear warnings, the Traffic alert and Collision Avoidance System (TCAS) and the Ground Proximity Warning System (GPWS) (United Airlines, 1998). The prevalence of cockpit alerting systems is also shown by their involvement in an increasingly comprehensive range of the pilot's tasks.

This increasing prevalence corresponds with the increasing capability of modern alerting systems. While simple alerting systems – detectors of a signal from a sensor – still abound, the most modern alerting systems may have input from multiple sensors and communications from other aircraft or the ground, and these inputs may be analysed by the alerting system using computationally intensive algorithms and large knowledge databases.

The role(s) of the cockpit alerting system have multiplied. This may be partly in response to their increased capabilities. Also, pilot familiarity with alerting systems changes the authority they allow the alerting system to have over them, ranging from a cessation of monitoring ('the alerting system will catch problems') to ignoring alerts ('the darn thing is wrong most of the time'). Finally, alerting systems maybe used in hitherto unintended situations, such as the stall warning becoming a cue to follow in high-performance manoeuvres.

In short, cockpit alerting systems have taken on a wide-range of roles beyond the attention-director role normally covered in the research literature. Describing these roles can be difficult to frame in 'automation' terms. Alerting systems are simultaneously highly and loosely automated: highly automated in that they are always monitoring and appear, from the pilot's point of view, to self-activate; loosely automated in that all but the most sophisticated can't actually control any aspect of the environment other than providing output to the pilot. Also, many alerting systems are considered safety-systems, whose actual role vis-à-vis the pilot, unlike an autopilot or flight management system, does not evolve through extended interaction in day-to-day operations but rather is selected by the pilot in the face of looming hazards.

This paper reviews the roles that cockpit alerting systems may assume, how these roles have changed with technological capability, and how effectively these roles allow alerting systems to function as pilot aids and safety systems. First, a denotation for alerting systems is proposed and contrasted with current connotations. A brief review of the technical considerations underlying alerting system design is provided. Then, the variety of roles of alerting systems noted both in the research literature and in studies of current operations are detailed. Finally, potential problems – and solutions – implied by these roles are discussed.

Denotation and connation of alerting systems

No industry standard definition of alerting systems exists which covers the full extent of current implementations. Formal definitions of automation typically imply the need for a level of control over the environment that the alerting system does not have (e.g. Sheridan, 1992, p. 3), or for novelty in having a machine involved in the task (e.g. Parasuraman and Riley, 1997, p. 231). This paper proposes the following formal denotation:

'An alerting system is an electro-mechanical system capable of monitoring for, detecting and announcing conditions anticipated (by the operator or the system designer) to impact the operator's near-term activities.'

While separate and different meanings are sometimes created for terms like *warning*, *alert*, and *alarm*, this definition does not create any distinction between them, while leaving room for implementation-specific meanings based on priority, likelihood or time-horizon (e.g. Sorkin, Kantowitz and Kantowitz, 1988; Veitengruber, 1977).

In contrasting this definition with the implicit use of the term 'alerting-system' in the literature, it is possible to illustrate alerting system qualities that have been well – and not-so-well – studied. For example, alerting systems are often thought of as safety systems, assisting the pilot in hazardous conditions (e.g. Riley et al, 1996), but they also may be used by the pilot as a desired cue, such as the stall warning during slow-flight training.

Likewise, alerting systems are often associated with aural alerts. However, the presence of an aural tone does not necessarily represent an alerting system (a crew-call sound, for example, may represent a signal rather than an alert), and an alerting system may not necessarily require an aural sound, but instead provide pop-up displays, warning lights, or tactile sensations.

Some traditional alerting systems have evolved to capabilities that include more than just alerting, yet remain in common parlance 'alerting systems'. For example, both TCAS and GPWS have executive capabilities, in that they can command the pilot to execute avoidance manoeuvres, and, in systems under test, automatically initiate manoeuvres. Although they may have outgrown the limited function of an alerting system, common connotations still refer to them as such.

Technical considerations in designing alerting systems

In designing an alerting system, fundamental decisions determine its capabilities, and by extension, the roles it can assume. This section briefly describes these design decisions, starting with the simplest alerting systems, signal detectors, and moving on to the more sophisticated systems, hazard detectors and hazard resolvers.

Signal detectors

The simplest alerting systems act as *signal detectors*, shown schematically in figure 1. The alerting system monitors a sensor input; when the input passes a threshold, an announcement is given to the pilot. Typically, the sensor input is also available to the pilot; as such, the alerting system has a direct correlate with a persistent display before the pilot, and may be thought of as an automated equivalent of a 'red-line'.

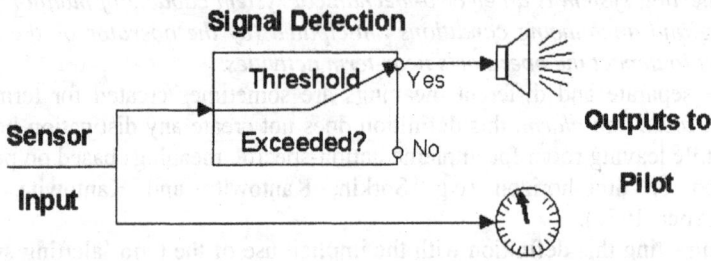

Figure 1 Schematic of signal detector

The threshold may be set in one of two ways. First, the alert threshold may be set by the alerting system operator with each use. This is common in domains where context sensitivities are important in determining the threshold, such as medicine. Such operator-determined alert thresholds can be found in aviation in less standardised operations such as general aviation. Not only may resourceful pilots implement their own simple alerting systems, but watch alarms and count-down-timers are common equipment for single-pilot Instrument Flight Rules (IFR) operations.

Conversely, the threshold may be set by the system designer when creating the alerting system, as is the case for the majority of aviation systems. The designer can build the alerting system around knowledge of sensor dynamics. For example, in developing an engine-fire alerting system from an engine temperature sensor, engineering analysis can identify the temperature readings expected during normal operations and the start of a fire. Also, pre-specified thresholds provide standardisation across a fleet of aircraft and multiple-person flight crews.

Selecting an alerting threshold is commonly described as a signal detection problem. The sensor's signal is presumed to be centred on one value if a condition exists, and another value if the condition does not exist; the signal varies around these values due to uncertainties, represented as noise. Hence, the threshold for detecting the existence of a condition mirrors statistical tests with their commensurate power to make correct detections and correct rejections, as well as their susceptibility to type I errors (missed detections) and type II errors (false alarms). At its heart, alerting remains a probabilistic venture, with the rates of missed detections and false alarms providing the core measure of alerting system efficacy.

An alerting system is limited by the ability of its sensor to observe the dynamics of interest. It is rare that a sensor provides a perfect assessment. Adding identical redundant sensors generally helps reduce the uncertainty bound, but also imposes more cost, weight, and potential for individual sensor failures. Sensors also indicate current values, whereas many thresholds must be set low enough to catch catastrophic conditions before they occur; such predictions therefore add extra uncertainty due to environmental unpredictability.

The trade-offs involved in the selection of an alerting threshold can be represented by a System Operating Characteristics curve (SOC), illustrated in figure 2. For a given sensor, a curve can be drawn that represents the loci of performance over all possible threshold settings. The SOC curves shown in figure 2 are smooth; in reality, they may have sudden jumps, such as with the TCAS SOC curves assembled by Kuchar (1996).

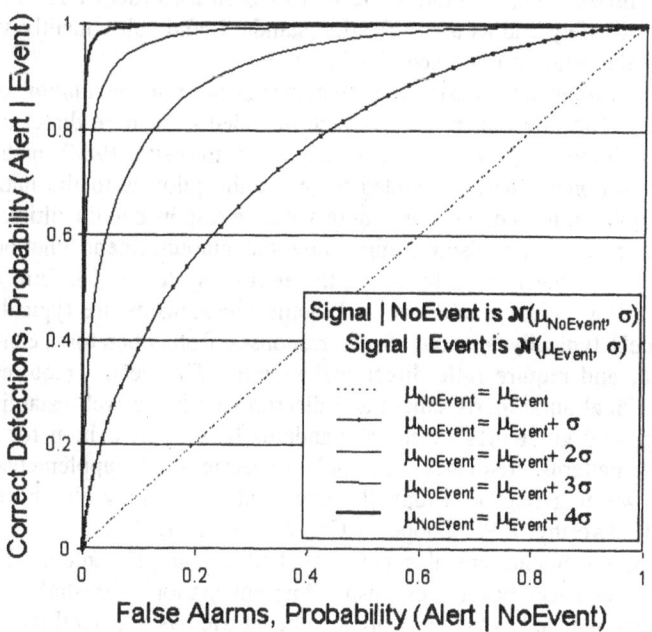

Figure 2 Representative system operating characteristics (SOC) curve

For systems evaluating, yes-or-no, whether a condition exists, the SOC directly portrays the factors to be considered in selecting a threshold. However, for continuously-evolving hazards, the factor of alert lead time is also an important consideration. For example, perfect yes-or-no detection of engine problems can be given by waiting until the engine fails; however, such an alerting system would be of limited use to the pilot. It is also useful to consider *when* an alert will go off; this may be measured by factors such as alert lead time (Bilimoria, 1998) or by the percentage of late alarms (alerts too late for an effective resolution) and the percentage of false alarms that will result in caused accidents.

Various mechanisms have been suggested for choosing the 'best' alerting threshold (e.g. Kuchar, 1996; Faitakis, Thapliyal and Kantor, 1998). A utility model is commonly used which considers the relative costs of false alarms (and caused accidents) versus missed detections (and late alarms), and finds the threshold value that minimises the expected cost. Quantifying these costs, however, can be difficult. Not only may it be controversial to assign a less-than-infinite cost to missed detections, but determining the cost of a false alarm can be problematic, due to its impact on day-to-day operations as well as its cumulative effects on pilot trust and non-conformance. Instead, in aviation it is common for an allowable missed detection rate to be set (often on the order of 10^{-3} to 10^{-9}) as an indicator of safety and as a certification standard, and subsequently verifying that the false alarm rate is not 'excessive.'

A common variant on a basic signal detector is the implementation of multi-phased alerts. The different phases may be intended as a more direct means of presenting likelihood (e.g. Sorkin, Kantowitz and Kantowitz, 1988), or they may serve as precautionary alerts, intended to prime the pilot as to the nature of a developing problem for a quicker and more accurate response to the ultimate alert.

Substantial research has also examined how the announcement function is best carried out; i.e. the mechanism by which the alerting system can inform the pilot of an event. For saliency, auditory and tactile mechanisms are typically used. These channels typically generate faster responses from operators, can convey urgency well, and require little directional search. The design requirement of making individual aural alerts salient and discriminate has a well-established set of knowledge and guidelines. General standards have been written for volume, length, on/off patterns, frequency, and spoken messages. A supplemental visual indication – warning flag on a dial, flashing light, etc. – may also be included (Stanton and Edworthy, 1999; Cooper, 1978; Veitengruber, 1977).

Tactile announcements are also being studied and implemented. The most common include stick-shaker/stick-pusher implementations for stall protection. Simple buzzers attached to the body are also being tried as a general indication to the pilot of events such as autopilot mode switches (Sklar and Sarter, 2000). The full extent to which tactile presentations can be used in operational environments remains an interesting topic of study.

In addition to their individual presentations, alerts need also be salient and discriminatable when multiple alerts are triggered at the same time. A range of conditions may trigger simultaneous alerts that will overlap to the extent that none can be distinguished. For example, in medicine, situations have been reported where over 20 alarms may trigger simultaneously (Meredith and Edworthy, 1994). Similar cases have been found in the nuclear power industry, process control, and, historically, in aviation (Woods, 1995; Cooper, 1978). As such, the technical capability represented by fully integrated cockpit systems is now being exercised to prioritise alerts and present them singly and sequentially (Proctor, 1998). This is less true in operations such as general aviation, where increasingly powerful alerting systems are now available but remain federated, preventing a central alert prioritisation scheme.

Hazard detectors

More complex alerting systems act as *hazard detectors*. Like signal detectors, they detect when a signal crosses a threshold; the difference is in what that signal represents. As shown in figure 3, multiple sensor signals feed into a pre-process that explicitly or implicitly derives a measure of 'hazard', which is then tested against a pre-specified hazard threshold. All, some or none of these sensor signals may also be available to the pilot.

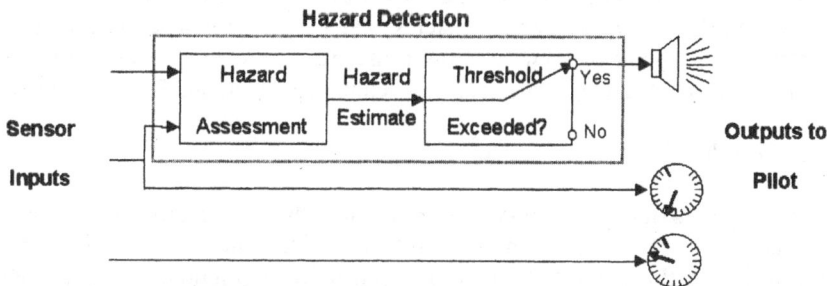

Figure 3 Schematic of a hazard detector

Such a design adds new challenges – namely, selection of a hazard metric and the means by which to calculate it. A common metric is projected time-to-accident. For example, both TCAS and GPWS calculate a projected time-to-impact; if it is less than an allowable threshold, then an alert is given. Another metric for assessing hazard is a direct prediction of hazard probability (e.g. Yang and Kuchar, 1997; Winder and Kuchar, 2000), representing one of several different things: the probability that an event is taking place; the probability that an event will occur if nothing is done; and the probability than an accident will occur if a standard resolution is effected (note that the probability threshold in this third case is normally quite small!).

12 *Amy R. Pritchett*

The calculations assessing the hazard can be quite intricate. For example, TCAS's only sensor input about the vertical position of traffic is digitally-transmitted altitude rounded to the nearest 100 feet, updated approximately once per second. Through filtering algorithms and storing the measurements from the last several updates, estimates of both altitude and vertical speed are generated. Similar inaccuracies are found in the measurements in the horizontal plane, which software processing must address (RTCA, 1983). These algorithms can dramatically change the SOC curves, as was found with the dramatic reductions in false alarms enabled by software changes to TCAS (Klass, 1998). The on-board calculations may be made faster by pre-computing important values into a database, which the alerting system can then to refer to as a built-in knowledge base (Carpenter and Kuchar, 1997, Yang and Kuchar, 1997). Several different thresholds or alerting triggers may be considered (e.g. RTCA, 1983; Liu, Golborne, Bun and Bartel, 1998).

Some hazard detectors can act as diagnostic systems, in that they can also help identify the underlying cause of the hazard. In process control domains, for example, diagnosis can involve substantial reasoning about the causes of undesired conditions (Borndorff-Eccarius and Johannsen, 1993); this reasoning process can be sufficiently difficult that expert systems have been proposed (e.g., Stanton and Baber, 1995). Similar systems have been tried in aviation, although, from the pilot's point of view, the root-cause of the problem is not always as important as knowledge of a safe course of action (e.g. Davis and Pritchett, 1999).

Hazard resolvers

The most sophisticated safety systems have more than just alerting capabilities: they can also act as *hazard resolvers*. In this case, the purpose of the alert is to direct the attention of the pilot to a commanded resolution calculated and displayed by the system, as shown in figure 4. Aural alerts themselves may contain information, such as the climb or descend commands given by TCAS. Likewise, systems may identify specific configuration actions to take: for example, in the case of a fuel imbalance, a system could provide the pilot with a specific set of fuel feed settings to implement.

Such hazard resolvers are currently established for hazards which develop more fluidly and for which an exact, detailed procedure can not be pre-specified. For example, aircraft collision avoidance requires manoeuvres to be developed on the fly; TCAS additionally communicates with the other aircraft to agree on which direction each aircraft will go. In calculating these avoidance manoeuvres, assumptions must be made about pilot behaviour. For example, TCAS assumes that the pilot will follow a command within five seconds and will execute a 0.25 g pull-up or push-over, as commanded (RTCA, 1983).

Because the alerting and resolution tasks are intrinsically linked, there are benefits to combining them inside the same box. By knowing what the resolution will be, the system can delay the alert until that resolution is appropriate, potentially reducing false alarms, while also ensuring that the alert is early enough for an effective resolution. Likewise, at the point of an alert, much of the information needed for a resolution calculation is already available.

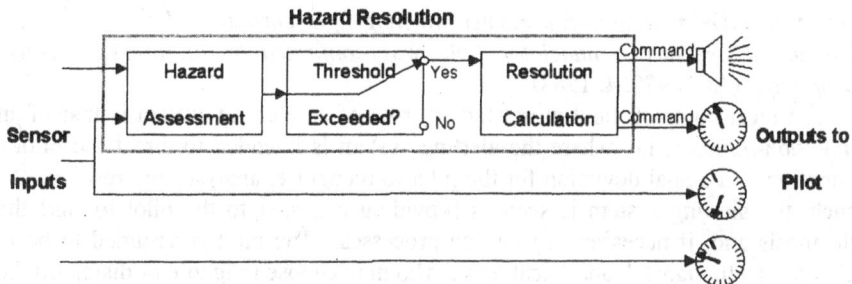

Figure 4 Schematic of hazard resolver

Once the system is capable of calculating a resolution, it is not a significant technical leap to give the alerting system control over the aircraft to enact the resolution (although it may be a practical problem in terms of cost, weight, and certification). Such systems are already being tested in the military for auto-ground collision avoidance (Scott, 1999), as well as being inherent parts of some flight control systems, such as the Airbus envelope protection systems.

Alerting system roles

Many different cockpit systems of varying sophistication may be denoted (or connoted) as alerting systems, and collectively they can perform a variety of roles. These roles may be categorised by their responses to the following questions:
- What will the pilot do in response to the alert? (From the point of view of the system designer, the certificator, the designer of the crew procedures, or the pilot).
- What does the alerting system provide to the pilot – a simple signal verifiable by the pilot, or a determination of hazard or required action?
- Will the pilot try to avoid the alert, or try to get the alert to occur?

The pilot can allow an alerting system to have a number of different roles. Some of these roles were motivation to create the alerting system in the first place; others are more likely post-hoc capitalisation on the alerting system's capabilities; and others may be unwanted outcomes of negative experiences. With the increase in technical capability also comes the potential for new, more authoritative roles for alerting systems. The following sections outline the range of alerting system roles, starting with those associated with the simplest systems and ending with those achievable only with the most technologically advanced.

Alerting system role: attention-director

'DFW to LAW experienced a master warning light enroute to LAW. The right engine oil pressure annunciator light was confirmed by oil pressure gauge dropping.' (ACN 97054, 1988).[1]

The most common (and most studied) role of an alerting system is that of an *attention-director*; i.e. where the alerting system is intended to direct the pilot's attention to a signal deviation for the pilot to recognise, analyse, and resolve. As such, the alerting system is seen as providing a trigger to the pilot to start the diagnosis and, if necessary, resolution processes. The pilot is assumed to be in charge as a thoughtful, analytical being who may choose to ignore or disregard the alert based on experience or knowledge of other aspects of current context.

This attention-directing role brings to the cockpit a continual monitoring capability that the pilot can not provide. Beyond concerns with the boredom and fatigue of asking a human operator to continually monitor a signal, humans have been found to sample signals at a rate scaled to the frequency with which they change; so-called 'complacency' may actually be seen as a reasonable and approximating-rational coping mechanism in the face of competing workload demands (Kerstholt, Passenier, Houttuin and Schuffel, 1996; Molloy and Parasuraman, 1996; Parasuraman et al, 1996). As such, alerting systems can particularly aid the pilot in detecting a number of conditions: rare changes in the signal; sudden, quickly evolving signal changes that might develop between pilot samples; and signals revealing particularly catastrophic or irreversible conditions whose high cost merit a dedicated monitor.

Just as engineers use signal detection theory to analyse alerting systems, so has it been applied to modelling human behaviour. Such a model has had a strong empirical fit in laboratory studies. In these studies it was noted that subjects may tend to adjust their sensitivity to 'cancel' the alerting system: for example, subjects were found to respond later to earlier alerts, rather than following alerts with a fixed reaction time (Elvers and Elrif, 1997; Sorkin and Woods, 1985; Getty, Swets and Pickett, 1994; See et al, 1997).

Beyond signal detection theory, several other models of human event detection have been proposed (e.g., Rouse, 1983). Some of these – error and error rate thresholds, and Kalman filters with residual error tests – mirror engineering models sometimes used to design alerting system algorithms. Other models, such

---

[1] Pilot report to the Aviation Safety Reporting System (ASRS), identified by report accession number and year.

as pattern recognition and judgement analysis, are intended for analysing expert behaviour in naturalistic environments.

While models of human event detection have been found fit well in laboratory tests, their predictive power for safety analysis of an aviation alerting system is limited for two significant reasons. First, the choice of 'mode' of behaviour is a pilot's opportunistic response to the full demands of the environment at the time of the alert, and is therefore hard to predict. Second, it is near-impossible to replicate in the laboratory the actual costs of the alert / no-alert decision. Laboratory studies need to create the ecology of the situation and tell their subjects the relative costs of a missed detection and false alarm; as such they can not reveal situations where an alerting system design varies in implicit-cost modelling from what the pilot would accept (Getty, Swets and Pickett, 1994).

This alerting system role is also characterised by what it does not do for the pilot. Dealing with an emergency might be characterised as a three-stage process: detection, diagnosis, and resolution (Rouse, 1983; Marshall and Baker, 1994). Obviously, an attention-director helps only with the first stage; subsequent steps are left to the pilot.

Alerting system role: nuisance

'I'm afraid the numerous false alarms, worse yet, the verbal distraction during critical phases, will cause the pilots to disarm [TCAS].' (ACN 171821, 1991).

'The fire warning was false but occurred at a point in the flight where it was most likely, a hot day under load during engine start. Given the extreme seriousness of fire and no time for a lengthy verification of the warning, the evac was necessary.' (ACN 114636, 1989).

Alerting systems are typically viewed as safety systems installed to detect events that the pilot might otherwise not catch. With this emphasis on preventing high cost missed detections, the alerting threshold is typically set to a value which has extremely few missed detections, at the expense of potentially having a high false alarm rate. As a result, many alerting systems have become notorious for their false alarms and are sometimes viewed as a *nuisance*.

Engine indications, for example, have historically been viewed by pilots with a fair amount of scepticism. Also, TCAS and GPWS have also been reported by pilots as having a detrimental false alarm rate (Mellone, 1993; Hasse, 1992, Vallauri, 1995; Wiener and Curry, 1980). Problems with high false alarm rates are not unique to aviation, but can also be found in medicine, in process control, and in other forms of transportation, including trains and automobiles (Parasuraman and Riley, 1997; Dingus et al, 1997).

This high false alarm rate may be attributable to several factors. First and foremost, it is often a necessary consequence of setting the alerting system threshold to meet 'hard' missed detection standards. Additionally, designers may not have anticipated the range of extraneous conditions which lead to false alarms.

For example, with engine fire alerting systems, several conditions may cause false alarms, such as extended ground idling, hot weather, and broken sensors or connectors (which may be more faulty than the engine itself).

Another factor contributing to a high false alarm rate is a poor understanding, on the part of the designer, of the true cost of a false alarm. As an isolated case a false alarm does not appear to have a high cost; other than requiring a diversion from the original flight plan, it seems like a safe move to avoid a potential catastrophe. Not until viewed in a longer-term sense does the true cost of false alarms come clear. While it is intended that the pilot should be able to disregard or over-ride the alerting system, he or she can not do so until they have regarded it sufficiently to decide that it is erroneous (Woods, 1995). If a pilot to chooses the follow a false alarm, then it has obstructed the outcome of the flight. If false alarms are frequent, then they can also start to obstruct the normal course of operations. For example, due to false GPWS alarms on approach to Cincinnati's runway 18L, special additions have been added to some airlines' briefings about conditions under which a GPWS alert may be disregarded for that approach.

For these reasons, false alarms can become such a nuisance that pilots may cease to respond, delay their response, turn off the alerting system, or discredit them to the extent that they ignore a correct detection. This so-called 'cry-wolf' phenomenon has been widely noted (e.g. Block, Nuutinen and Ballasts, 1999; Seminara, Gonzalez and Parsons 1997; Weiner and Curry, 1980; Paté-Cornell, 1986).

Alerting system role: final authority on problem

'It was possibly a false TCAS II alert, but like the GPWS, it's better to be safe than sorry.' (ACN 163373, 1990).

'... in IMC conditions the mode 2 GPWS warning occurred for 2 cycles. We immediately initiated climb to 8000 feet... After landing we phoned air traffic control and they became very defensive, assuring us that their minimum vector altitudes had not been violated...It was not a case of obvious false warning so we could not just disregard it, yet ATC was offended! We're alive!' (ACN 159794, 1990).

Just as a pilot may over-rely on the alerting system by not monitoring, so too may he or she 'catch' an oncoming problem before the alert, but rely on the alert as a *final authority on the problem*. For example, a pilot may notice that engine temperature is increasing. Uncertain whether the gauge is wrong and whether the problem warrants immediate action, the pilot may not take any drastic action until the problem is clearly defined. An alert provides that definition.

Likewise, the pilot may be reluctant to act based on uncertain information on matters over which he or she does not have complete authority. For example, Midkiff and Hansman (1993) found that pilots were reluctant to act based on overheard voice communications about possible traffic conflicts. In such situations, the air traffic controller normally has authority over the pilot's actions. However, a TCAS advisory provides the pilot with the authority to act.

Alerting system role: trusted monitor

Just as pilots may under-rely on an alert when it is triggered, so may they over-rely on the alerting system as a *trusted monitor* when all appears to be going well, an effect Wiener and Curry (1980) termed 'primary-backup inversion.' The designer of an alerting system generally has an image of the role the pilot should play in monitoring independent of the alerting system. This intended role may vary: some alerting systems intend that the pilot should continue to monitor as before; others, such as with the dark cockpit philosophy, intend to take over much of the monitoring role, but still intend that the pilot should keep a general awareness of the flight and be observant for anomalies.

This over-reliance when all is going well may be correlated with under-reliance when an alert is given. Through nuisance alerts and system descriptions, the pilot may be well-convinced that the system's monitoring is continuous, albeit with conservative alerting criteria. While alerting systems are often thought of as interacting with the pilot when they activate, this role highlights how the presence of an alerting system can change patterns of behaviour in normal conditions in which the alerting system is silent.

Alerting system role: resolution assessor

'On climbout at approximately flight level 220, intermittent #1 engine overheat light on, followed by intermittent red fire handle light and bell. When throttle closed, all warning indications ceased. Initiated return to LAX. Later in descent all afore-mentioned indications returned. Shut down engine #1 and fired left extinguisher bottle... All warning indications ceased. Still further in descent same warning indications returned. Fired right extinguisher bottle. Indications again ceased. Landing at LAX uneventful.' (ACN 118275, 1989).

Most alerting systems, namely signal and hazard detectors, are thought of as providing an alert that an undesired event is occurring. Additionally, however, the disappearance of the alert can serve as a tool for assessing when this condition has been resolved; i.e. act as a *resolution-assessor* (e.g. Stanton and Baber, 1995). For example, consider the generation of an engine temperature warning. Not only does it indicate a potential problem with the engine, but it may also be a useful tool in resolving the problem – namely, the alert can let the pilot know whether throttling back the engine is sufficient, or whether more extreme action is needed.

Signal and hazard detectors do not provide open-loop guidance to the pilot about a resolution (i.e. they do not say 'do this and everything will be ok'). Instead, their alerts may be viewed as a feedback mechanism that lets pilots know the results of their efforts. This closed-loop process may be undertaken by the pilot in a deliberate, purposeful manner. Conversely, this process can also conceivably be undertaken in frustration (i.e. 'hit every button until the darn alert goes away').

In many situations this role of an alerting system can be positive in helping the pilot resolve a hazard quickly. Correspondingly, it suggests the danger of extending this alerting system role too far. Rather than viewing his or her task as keeping away from alerts, in most situations it is preferable for the pilot to view his or her role as keeping the aircraft near the desired condition, and to recognise that the absence of an alert does not imply the situation is completely satisfactory.

Alerting system role: desired cue

Normally, an alert is something to be avoided when possible, and resolved when necessary. However, in some cases a system's alert may become a *desired cue*. For example, consider the stall warning. Implemented on the vast majority of aircraft flying today, it was initially motivated by a desire to alert the pilot when near an inadvertent stall and spin. However, most pilots trained on light general aviation aircraft are quickly introduced to another use for the stall warning – namely as a cue during slow flight training that the aircraft is truly just above stall speed, which the pilot should seek to keep on. This stall warning is also typically a desired cue when landing a light aircraft; if triggered with the wheels just off the ground, then it is a sign to all on board that the touchdown occurred properly just above stall.

This role of desired cue can even be capitalised upon explicitly in operating procedures. For example, current airline windshear avoidance procedures typically call for full-power and for the pilot to pull back on the flight controls until the onset of the stick-shaker (a tactile stall warning). Not only does it reduce the visual workload of the pilot, but it also provides a consistent cue during even the most extreme windshear events, in which aircraft airspeed indications may fluctuate rapidly in response to rapidly changing wind speeds. The role of desired cue has become sufficiently common in industry that other envelope-protection alerting systems have been proposed specifically for this role (e.g., Horn, 1999).

The use of cockpit alerts as a desired cue is made possible by a built-in safety margin. For example, stall warnings commonly trigger before stall; flap overspeed warnings initiate at 10 knots below the actual limit; and red-line alerts on airspeeds and engine speeds have a built in safety-margin of about 10%. As such, pilots often construe alerts as marking achievable – but not exceedable – flight conditions.

This role of alerting systems has evolved through pilot experience and, perhaps, with a perceived need for the cues they can provide. This evolution may be judged as having reached the point where this role is reinforced by training and procedures, and where the alerting system is used in response to situations beyond those it was originally intended to protect against.

Alerting system role: task management aid

The most wide-spread connotation of alerting systems is that they guard against unanticipated, hazardous conditions. However, in some situations alerts are anticipated and serve to direct the pilot's attention from one planned task to another (e.g. Hickling, 1994). In such cases, alerting systems can fill the role of *task management aids*. This role is illustrated by the use of watch alarms and timers in single-pilot Instrument Flight Rules (IFR) operations. The pilot may specifically choose to set the timer throughout the flight. It can be used to alert the pilot that something new needs to be started (e.g. radio call of waypoint passage), that something needs to be ended (e.g. the conclusion of a timed approach), that something needs to be checked (e.g. periodic reminders to check the aircraft systems' status), or that something ought to be happening (e.g. reaching an 'expect further clearance' time).

Such alerts can also be found in more sophisticated cockpits: for example, the 1000 feet-to-go horn alerts the pilot that he or she (or the autopilot) is transitioning into a level altitude. This role varies from the common conception of an alert – it is more mundane and less focused on emergencies. However, it does highlight the extent to which alerts may be not only expected, but can be cues within a pilot's plan.

Alerting system role: overload

'I find it very disturbing that a warning system like the GPWS can be allowed to disrupt air traffic control and cockpit communications because of its loud volume and its inability to be shut off.' (ACN 254544, 1993).

While an alerting system is normally intended to direct a pilot's attention to a problem, there are cases where an alert instead serves to *overload* the pilot and obstruct piloting tasks. Sometimes this overload may be purely physical in nature – due to the volume of the alert or the extreme brightness of a warning light, the pilot may not be able to recognise anything beyond the existence of the alert. For example, pilot reports filed with the Aviation Safety Reporting System (ASRS) have cited TCAS as the distraction precipitating unauthorised landings at Atlanta, Newark, and Salt Lake City (ACN 168712, 1991; ACN 178850, 1991; ACN 179521, 1991). This overload may also be more cognitive in nature. Because of the alert's saliency, the pilot may find it hard to ignore the alert (Mosier, 1996) and may prioritise the alert's subject before more important tasks, negating any task management and planning the pilot may have performed.

This overload may also occur in the presence of multiple alerts and many steps have been taken in aviation to resolve it, including allowing the pilot to silence some types of alerts, and prioritising and sequentially presenting alerts through a central alert-integration scheme (Proctor, 1998). While reducing overload, this solution has not proven able to totally prevent it. For example, in describing a recent crash of an MD-81, the co-pilot gave the following description:

'All the lamps are blinking and there are a lot of warning sounds in the cockpit. It is really a terrible environment. It is not possible to manage all this information. With so many malfunctions you stop analyzing them and concentrate on the flying. That's the only thing to do.' (Mårtensson, 1995, p. 315).

Integration is not an available solution for all aircraft. For example, sophisticated cockpit systems are now sufficiently affordable for general aviation. However, such systems are typically federated, i.e. they are independent units that do not co-ordinate their functions with other cockpit systems. With such installations the potential is growing for multiple alerts to create pilot overload.

Alerting system role: initiator of procedures

'Southbound approximately 80 nm north of ATL at flight level 290, the #2 fire warning activated. Engine was shutdown in accordance with emergency procedures and the flight diverted into ATL Hartsfield airport without further incident. To the best of my knowledge the warning was a false indication, but procedures required an immediate landing, which I did.' (ACN 89906, 1988).

The attention-director role assumes that the pilot will follow a fluid, cognitive diagnostic process in assessing the cause of an alert and the solution to the problem it identifies. In many operations, however, the alerting system instead acts as an *initiator of procedures*. These procedures can lead pilots through the diagnostic and resolution processes in a manner that can benefit from *a priori* study of the most likely and most hazardous situations. Procedures can also help pilots incorporate the temporal dynamics of the situation, such as engine-failure procedures in light aircraft that start with the potential resolutions requiring the most time to take effect (e.g. carb.-heat, fuel) and end with those with immediate effect (e.g. magnetos). If well-trained, pilots can use procedures to enact faster and more consistent reactions.

When alerting systems are intended to be initiators of procedures, there may be less of a desire for the alerting system to be given diagnostic and resolution capabilities, as these processes are built into the procedure. For example, in a flight simulator study of pilots' responses to onboard system failures, the pilots indicated few perceived benefits to enhanced alerting systems that presented diagnostic information in situations where a known procedure already existed (Davis and Pritchett, 1999).

The procedure can be a good way to actively draw the pilot into the diagnostic process. As an extreme example, the procedure following a fire-warning on the UH-60 'Blackhawk' helicopter has the pilot investigate the warning's veracity, including asking the crew-chief if there is smoke and monitoring the other gauges. In other words, the procedure can be a structure through which the pilot can verify the alert and evaluate the aircraft condition.

Conversely, in other situations the procedure may exist to essentially remove the pilot cognitively from the diagnosis and resolution task, and instead effect an autonomic response. In this situation, the alerting system has an executive role which is intended to require actions from pilots. For example, CFIT training material urges pilots to 'follow the GPWS alert'; likewise, with more reliable engine fire indications, pilots may be trained to activate the extinguishers without questioning.

Alerting system role: command device

'*Aircraft was not acquired visually until after evasive action was taken... TCAS and ATC saved the day. A collision would have occurred without the heads-up alert we got from TCAS.*' (ACN 179784, 1991).

'*The sequence of events transpired very fast – faster than you really can analyze the situation. The warnings and commands are very authoritative and you react almost out of fright.*' (ACN 165484, 1990).

A hazard-resolver-type alerting system may be implemented as a *command device*. In this role, the alerting system has an executive role in which pilots can be commanded, in real-time, to follow specific actions. For example, 'TCAS is a 'first' in a class of avionics that actually advises a manoeuvre, rather than the more conventional role of showing the situation to the pilot for his evaluation' (Williamson and Spencer, 1989, p. 1741). This implementation may be chosen when exact, specific procedures do not exist for every situation, and a resolution must instead be calculated on the fly; or this implementation and role may be chosen when there is a desire, by the alerting system designer, to reinforce a pre-specified procedure.

Within this alerting system role, it can be difficult – and sometimes undesired – for the pilot to become cognitively involved in the situation other than as an executor of the displayed commands. Not only may there be little time to delay, but also hazard-resolver alerting systems can be quite complex, making analysis of the reasoning behind the alert and commands difficult.

The pilot has two inter-related concepts to verify: the timing of the alert itself, and the substance of the subsequent resolution. The alerting system may have several different 'modes' of operation (such as the different thresholds and constraints on avoidance manoeuvres within TCAS as a function of altitude), and they may have several different alert triggers (such as GPWS, which has several different criteria that can trigger an alert). Most alerting systems do not present their underlying reasoning, so the pilot may not be aware of the assumptions and objectives underlying the system.

Also, from the pilot's point of view, the alerting system may now be presenting them with more than just information. Instead, the alerting system is now providing such a neat-and-tight package of information that it may be difficult to change their actions away from those commanded in any small way without the whole set unravelling. For example, TCAS not only calculates the projected efficacy of an avoidance manoeuvre on its own – it also communicates and co-ordinates with the other aircraft as to 'who goes where'. For a pilot to not-conform to a TCAS manoeuvre represents not just an over-ride of the command, but also the breaking of a hidden electronic contract made with the other aircraft.

In some sense, a safety system intended for this role may have advanced beyond the capabilities normally attributed to an alerting system. While it does generate alerts in response to hazardous situations, it also provides the analysis and command capability normally associated with other types of automation, such as expert systems, decision aids, and flight control systems.

Unlike many forms of advanced automation, however, the pilot is still physically involved in the control loop. Practical reasons for leaving the pilot in the control loop include concerns about the complexity and cost of creating, certifying and implementing a fully-automatic system, especially as an add-on into established cockpits. Also, the alerting system, as with automation in general, is often recognised as needing the pilot to assess its appropriateness within the current context (e.g. Rogers, Schutte and Latorella, 1996).

However, the decision to leave the pilot in the control loop may have an evolutionary explanation as well: current command device roles have evolved from roles associated with simpler alerting systems, in which the pilot has always been a fundamental part of the decision process. By leaving the pilot in the loop, there is often the appearance of the pilot remaining as the final authority in what action will be taken; however, with some systems this authority may not be balanced by the pilot having the ability to verify or question the alerting system due to time, workload, system complexity and lack of information.

With this alerting system role, pilots are typically measured as an actuator: i.e. by their reaction-time and command-following accuracy. For example, in recent tests of an automatic ground collision avoidance system (Auto-GCAS) for fighters, the following was noted:

'Because pilots are adamant about having final authority over their aircraft, the [flight test] team initially gave the pilot an ability to always override the Auto-GCAS. Extensive testing, plus discussion with F-22 test pilots, changed that attitude. During all-terrain testing, we found that even the slightest override of the GCAS autopilot in the wrong direction would blast you through the [minimum safe altitude] floor.' (Scott, 1999).

Potential problems with alerting systems roles

The just-completed review of alerting system roles revealed the good, the bad, and the unexpected. While alerting systems often meet their intended roles, they are also commonly ignored, used in unintended ways, and misunderstood. This section will discuss the problematic implications of the alerting system roles just described.

Problem: alerting systems function differently from other forms of cockpit automation

Alerting systems have a unique position in the cockpit, as they are often viewed as 'safety systems' intended to help the pilot predict, avoid and resolve hazardous situations. As such, several facets of discussions on automation design do not carry over well to alerting systems. For example, Woods (1986) suggested that 'good' automation would create a diverse, joint human-machine cognitive system; however, as a back-up monitor, alerting systems are inherently a redundant system performing many of the same monitoring, detection and diagnosis actions as the pilot. Likewise, 'normal' cockpit automation is activated and de-activated by the pilot. With this control, the pilot is comparatively free to determine his or her own fluid approach to the tasks at hand. Alerting systems are intended to disrupt this fluid process; they can not even be purposefully ignored without first requiring attention (Woods, 1995).

High pilot workload is generally considered undesirable. As such, reducing workload is generally a motivation for automation, and guidelines for designing automation for this purpose have been developed (e.g. Kantowitz and Caspar, 1988). In fact, the pejorative term *clumsy automation* has been applied to systems that require attention or increase workload at times when the pilot is already under high-workload and time-criticality (Weiner, 1989). Unfortunately, given that they are intended to activate in hazardous situations and demand attention, many alerting systems are fundamentally and irrevocably clumsy automation. At best, steps can be taken to reduce the potential for pilot overload through alert prioritisation (Proctor, 1998).

As such, much of the research and operational literature on the design and use of automation can not be directly applied. Likewise, measures of 'good' interaction with automation may not match measures commonly used for an alerting system. These differences are rooted in differences between 'efficiency' measures such as average performance and workload, and 'safety' measures that examine the frequencies and costs of hazardous occurrences.

In the same way, common fixes to problems with automation are not as easily applied to problems with alerting systems. For example, pilots typically receive formal flight training in the use of both alerting systems and 'normal' cockpit automation. However, many pilots report that a higher level of confidence in, and understanding of, automation (most notably the Flight Management System [FMS]) develops with on-the-job experience. This may be viewed as both a process for accumulating understanding of the system itself, as well as adapting his or her skills to the new environment including the automation (Kirlik, 1993). However, a pilot does not receive the same on-the-job training with many alerting systems; they trigger so rarely that a pilot may see none, one or only a few in his or her career.

Problem: nuisance

'I don't know if you are tracking false GPWS warnings, but if you have any statistics I would like to see them. This system has given me enough false indications over the last five years, that I am suspect of its value to me or the flight deck.' (ACN 202795, 1992).

As noted earlier, alerting systems may take on the role of a nuisance, generally because of their high false alarm rate. This is obviously a problem, and one that can not be easily solved. An alerting system's fundamental limits (as illustrated by the false alarm – missed detection trade-off described by its SOC curve) are largely determined by its sensors and algorithms, and by environmental unpredictability. Ultimately, the best results will be attained through the use of the most accurate sensors and alerting algorithms. For example, significant reductions in false ground proximity warnings have been enabled through the Enhanced Ground Proximity Warning System's (EGPWS) inclusion of terrain databases as a reference for alerts, as compared to the older GPWS's ability to only consider radar altitude.

Within an alerting system's limits, it has been suggested that the base rate of the event should be considered, such that the alert threshold can be set to maximise the probability that any alert is correct (e.g. Parasuraman, Hancock and Olofinboba, 1997; Bliss, Gilson and Deaton, 1995). While it is correct to re-evaluate how the alert thresholds are set (and to re-adjust the cost of a false alarm), their common role in aviation as safety systems requires more emphasis on a low rate of missed detections for certification and for acceptance by the pilot community.

Other potential solutions include making the alert less strident so that the pilot is not as violently disrupted from his or her task. As a related solution, some systems have established phased alerts where the precautionary-phase alerts are less strident and serve to 'gently' prepare the pilot for a subsequent diversion of their full attention.

A third potential solution is to examine the intended role of the alerting system. Alerts intended to take over the pilot's actions, such as those demanding the execution of commands or procedures, may be perceived as more of a nuisance than those that function as attention-directors. In other words, the costs of false alarms from more authoritative systems may be higher and should be considered during design.

Likewise, alerts whose underlying basis are harder to perceive may appear erratic to the pilot. In such cases, the alerting system may be tasked with explaining itself, so that it is perceived as a consistent – albeit conservative – entity, rather than as a spurious nuisance.

Problem: trust in the alerting system

'When you've read the horror stories of others for not following GPWS warnings, and you believe your position to be safe in relation to the ground, it creates a tough conflict when the GPWS issues such a warning (most likely a false one).' (ACN 202384, 1992).

'There is a great lack of confidence in the TCAS system with the pilot group. I was one of them but I believe this saved a mid-air collision.' (ACN 185690, 1991).

The trust a pilot places in a system has been demonstrated to have a strong effect on his or her interaction with it. Trust in automation is typically associated with the dependability and predictability the operator has experienced in using it (Lee and Moray, 1992). However, most alerting systems interact with the pilot so little that a different basis for trust is relied upon, termed 'faith' by Lee and Moray (1992) and 'fiduciary responsibility' by Muir (1987).

Fiduciary responsibility is a measure of system capability inferred from certification by some outside, respected authority. It has the potential to provide a fair assessment of trust during the pilot's first interaction with an alerting system. However, it is extremely brittle to any perception of ill performance; trust in an alerting system be seriously damaged by a missed detection or false alarm. Once trust has been reduced to a level lower than justified by the performance of the system, it can be very hard to restore (Muir, 1994). This type of trust is not based solely on personal interaction. For example, in the case of TCAS, not only have pilots passed on their experiences – good and bad – by word-of-mouth, but the popular press has broadcast both situations where TCAS 'saved-the-day' and reports insinuating TCAS is unsafe. Such reports can impact perceptions of fiduciary responsibility.

Trust alone does not solely determine how the system will be used. Among several factors is the operator's own self-confidence in their ability to assess the relevant hazard independently (Lee and Moray, 1994; Riley, 1996). The impact of trust and self-confidence on pilot interaction with an alerting system is shown conceptually in figure 5. Each is broken down into two levels, high and low, representing four possible quadrants. When pilot self-confidence is high and his or her trust in the alerting system is low, it is reasonable to expect that the pilot will act primarily on his or her own assessment; when the pilot's self-confidence at the task is low and trust in the alerting system is high, then his or her action may be based primarily on the alerting system. Of note is the upper-left quadrant. Presumably we want the pilot to have both high self-confidence and high trust in the alerting system. However, in this condition, should a situation arise where the pilot not agree with the output of the alerting system, then he or she can be left in a conundrum about what actions to take, and it is impossible to predict with certainty what reasoning – the pilot's or the alerting system's – will determine the ultimate course of action.

		Pilot Self-Confidence at Task	
		High	Low
Trust in Alerting System	High	Indeterminate	Pilot will probably follow alerting system
	Low	Pilot will probably verify or ignore alerting system	Indeterminate

Figure 5 Trust in the alerting system and self-confidence as determinants of pilot action

Problem: alerting system complexity

As with other types of cockpit automation, pilot understanding of alerting systems may be difficult due to their complexity. The complexity of cockpit automation, especially Flight Management Systems (FMS), has been noted in many studies as an obstruction to good pilot understanding of the system. This complexity is often quantified in terms of the number of 'modes' within the system. While alerting systems may have modes in the form of context-sensitive alerting thresholds or multiple triggering criteria, a better measure of complexity – from the pilot's point of view – may be a rough categorisation of the amount of processing and fore-knowledge required to go from the information available to the pilot to the assessment made by the alerting system.

For simple signal detectors, this complexity measure would be very low – with a simple check of a gauge the pilot can verify the alerting system's output. At the other extreme are those hazard detectors and hazard resolvers that are intentionally designed for better overall performance than that expected from the pilot alone. Take TCAS, for example. Its alerts and commands are based on several processes not easily re-created by the pilot: memory of previous positions and convergence rates to estimate current conditions; filtering the assessment of convergence rate, tuned to the statistical properties of the sensor inputs; and communication with the intruding aeroplane to co-ordinate avoidance manoeuvres (RTCA, 1983). The logic to perform these calculations is intricate enough that specialised techniques had to be developed to certify its logic (e.g. Heimdahl, Leveson and Reese, 1998). Other alerting systems may also have built-in knowledge in the form of databases (Kuchar and Carpenter, 1997) or prioritisation schemes (Wiener and Curry, 1980; Proctor, 1998), adding to their apparent complexity.

Problem: presentation of feedforward and feedback information about the alerting system

Since the typical alerting system only provides visual and aural alerts – and possibly commands – its apparent functioning can be very 'opaque'; i.e. similar to effects found in studies of complex automated systems, the alerting system may not present the rationale, criteria, and determining factors for its actions to the operator to promote understanding (Sarter and Woods, 1992; Sarter and Woods, 1994; Hickling, 1994; Noyes and Starr, 2000).

An opaque interface with an alerting system may be solved by presenting more information about the alerting system's reasoning – such as a representation of the alerting system's threshold on a relevant situation display. Such *consonance* between an alerting system and a situation display can help pilots react in accordance with alerts that they might not otherwise agree with (Pritchett and Vandor, 1999). In creating such a consonant presentation, it is often important to have it available not just after the alert (when time can be critical), but also before the alert. Such a continuously-available display provides a predictive power found beneficial (Trujillo, 1994; Noyes, Cresswell–Starr and Rankin, 1999; Noyes and Starr, 2000). Such a predictive power may also serve as feedforward information about the alerting system, allowing it to interact in a less disruptive manner with the pilot's planning and task management.

Treating the pilot's reaction to alerts as a logical process, the pilot's ability to understand the alerting system determines his or her ability to assess the validity of its alert and commands. Likewise, improving the pilot's ability to understand the system also serves implicitly to train the pilot on the dynamics of the hazard, potentially increasing the performance of his or her own independent judgements. As such, providing a better interface into the alerting system's functioning can serve as a parallel, co-ordinated effort to make the pilot *understand* the alerting system and to *agree* with it, and by extension to allow the pilot to develop a better basis for trust.

This solution may also extend to problems noted earlier. Having the alerting system provide both feedback (once the alert has occurred) and feedforward (before the alert) may, by extension, help reduce the negative impacts of alerting system complexity and of nuisance alerts, while helping the pilots form an appropriate trust in the alerting system (Bliss, Jeans and Prioux, 1996).

However, the correct presentation of this information may require a fundamental change in the way situation displays – and situation awareness – are viewed relative to the alerting task. Pilots' need for situation awareness is widely recognised (Endsley, 1995). To meet this need, situation displays are being widely implemented to provide the pilot with a clear picture of many aspects of the environment, such as aircraft system status, terrain, weather and traffic. However, these displays typically support a situation assessment that is independent of the alerting system. For example, the terrain shown on situation displays associated with EGPWS are typically colour-coded based on altitude, which is not the same schemata used for generating alerts. Based on aircraft configuration and vertical speed, it may be possible for 'yellow' terrain to not generate an alert, or for an alert to be triggered by potential impact with terrain shown in green.

As such, complete situation awareness may need to include 'alerting system awareness'. This poses not only a requirement on the situation display to provide alerting system awareness, but also a limitation on the alerting system: in order to *communicate* the its functioning, the alerting system's logic must be *communicable*, limiting its allowable complexity (Bainbridge, 1983).

Problem: unintended roles

The capabilities of an alerting system may be capitalised upon in ways not intended by its designer or not substantially discussed in the research literature. Pilots may opportunistically use the alerting system as a desired cue, as a resolution-assessor, or as a task management aid. These unintended roles may even be institutionalised through operating procedures and flight training.

These additional roles may sometimes be viewed as a side-benefit of alerting systems. However, the alerting system designer has neither the same level of control over their emergence, nor the ability to tailor the system to meet their needs. They can be difficult to predict; only the most general principles can help estimate what unintended roles may occur, such as estimating potential pilot actions when given the information the alerting system brings to the cockpit (e.g. Vallauri, 1997), or as a result of risk homeostasis.

Given that these unintended roles may occur, they may place additional requirements on alerting system design. For example, because some alerting systems may be used as resolution assessors or desired cues, they may require a built-in margin of play so that aircraft operation near their thresholds represents an acceptable level of safety.

Problem: procedural conflicts

'We were getting a TCAS [command] and the approach controller told us to ignore the TCAS... It put us in quite a dilemma with TCAS telling us to do one thing and the controller telling us to do another.' (ACN 177004, 1991).

Associated with many alerting systems are operating procedures dictating how they shall be used. For example, executive alerting systems such as GPWS and TCAS typically mandate a prompt reaction to their alerts, followed by conformance to their commands to resolve the hazard. However, other procedures may interact with the alerting system's procedure.

These interactions may be direct conflicts: for example, while the procedure for GPWS calls for an immediate pull-up, approach procedures for specific runways (such as Cincinnati's approach to runway 18L) give a detailed description of situations in which the pilot may elect to ignore a GPWS alert. Likewise, these interactions may represent the operator's reluctance to override standard operating procedures: for example, pilots have reported receiving conflicting commands from air traffic controllers and TCAS about how to resolve a potential collision hazard (Mellone, 1993; Vallauri, 1995). Finally, these conflicts may also result from conflicting procedures associated with simultaneous alerts from different alerting systems.

Obviously, the potential for procedural conflicts requires careful consideration during the design and testing of the alerting system. Likewise, procedural conflicts may also require consideration during implementation of new standard operating procedures. For example, changes in air traffic control procedures, such as closely-spaced parallel approaches, now require study for their impact on TCAS alerts; in some cases it may be necessary for the pilot to set TCAS to a less-authoritative alerting-only mode to prevent conflicts.

Problem: over- and under-reliance on the alerting system

'I believe the TCAS saved our lives and in retrospect I wish I had followed its advisories more aggressively.' (ACN 176015, 1991).

'We all should look into developing procedures involving TCAS II and when and at what times it should be used.' (ACN 176392, 1991).

The creation of a more capable alerting system implies that the pilot can – or should – rely upon it to some degree. Actually creating this level of reliance, however, may be difficult. Examining automation in general, problems with under- and over-reliance have been cited in many different domains, including aircraft, railroad, ship, process control, and medicine (Riley, 1996; Parasurman and Riley, 1997; Mosier and Skitka, 1996; Guerlain, 1999).

Under-reliance on automation is comparatively rare – for systems used on a day-to-day basis, the system must usually demonstrate during testing that it will be useful to the pilot before it is implemented. Predicting the reliance on an alerting system, on the other hand, is difficult based only upon the artificial conditions under which it must be tested (Pritchett, Vándor and Edwards, 1999). Hence the significant rate of non-conformance to alerting systems is commonly cited as the most visible example of under-reliance to automation (Parasuraman and Riley, 1997; Wiener and Curry, 1980). For example, one study of ASRS reports involving TCAS found a self-reported rate of non-conformance of 16%, one half of which were listed as conscious decisions by pilots at the time that another action would be better or the alert should be ignored (Mellone, 1993). Studies of GPWS reported a very high rate (73%) of 'delayed pilot reactions' to terrain alerts, with 64% of responding pilots citing their opinions that corrective action should not be initiated without first attempting to verify the warning (Hasse, 1992).

Over-reliance on alerting systems has also been identified. With the simplest alerting systems, this may be manifested as primary-backup-inversion, in which pilot behaviour during normal monitoring is not as involved as the designer had intended. As systems become more capable – and more authoritative – this over-reliance may transition from occurring just during normal monitoring to also allowing the alerting system to effectively make decisions in the face of hazards, opening the door to errors of commission in which a pilot acts upon faulty guidance.

As with automation, no tried-and-true set of solutions to over- and under-reliance has yet been identified. Many solutions stem from solving the more basic problems already described. Having the alerting system provide more information about its functioning – and hence its limitations – may enable the pilot to assess the alert's correctness within the immediate context. Likewise, reductions in false alarms through better sensors and alerting algorithms may help reduce under-reliance through improving trust.

More importantly, a potential solution may be found in clearly-defining the level of reliance expected from the pilot. Without this knowledge the pilot may not be aware that his or her behaviour does not match that assumed by the system designer. Likewise, without this knowledge, other processes such as training and drafting of procedures may not support appropriate reliance. This potential solution parallels calls for a clear and consistent philosophy of use for cockpit automation.

Problem: authority/responsibility double bind

'None of us even had time to look at the TCAS scope to see the aircraft providing the conflict. All we did was follow the command on the vertical velocity indicator and audio warning to descend.' (ACN 174742, 1991).

Typical measures of automation authority rate the amount of actuation performed by the automation, and the extent to which this actuation is initiated by the pilot (e.g. Billings, 1997; Sheridan, 1992). With alerting systems, however, actuation is performed by the pilot as initiated by the alerting system. Therefore, common classifications of automation authority do not capture the authority of an alerting system. Instead, the authority of the alerting system may be categorised by the level of control it has over the pilot. The simplest signal-detector alerting system may control the pilot only by inducing him or her to consider a gauge reading. With hazard-detector and hazard-resolver systems, a high degree of authority stems from their ability to 'cognitively railroad' the pilot into decisions that he or she can't verify due to lack of time, excessive workload, not having the same information as the alerting system, or an inaccurate conception of how the alerting system arrives at its decisions.

Beyond the practical under- and over-reliance issues, situations in which the pilot is cognitively railroaded raise more philosophical concerns about a condition termed by Woods (1986) as the 'authority / responsibility double bind'. Ultimate responsibility for flight safety rests with the captain. Historically, a commensurate complete level of authority stemmed from his or her almost complete level of control over how the flight was executed, within the constraints imposed by aircraft performance, air traffic control, and regulations (and the latter two can be negotiated or broken when needed). While the pilot is still nominally in charge, increasingly powerful alerting systems are assuming authority over specific hazards. At an extreme, the pilot may be responsible for – and required to execute – actions over which they can no longer hold authority.

Conclusions

'What with GPWS, windshear alerters, TCAS alerts, gear horns, bell, buzzers, clackers and split seconds to absorb, process and react, maybe we should re-evaluate the addition of more technology into our cockpits and whether it really improves safety?' (ACN 181018, 1991).

Because there is no perfect alerting system, the decision to implement an alerting system can be controversial. Normal guidelines for automated systems need often be broken when designing an alerting system for the rare, the hazardous, and the unexpected. In implementing alerting systems, the aviation industry must consider the '60 Minutes Test',[2] in which we ponder which question, given the capabilities of the alerting system, we feel we could better substantiate in a TV news interview:

'Why didn't you implement this alerting system earlier if it could have prevented an accident?'

or

'Why did you implement this alerting system when you knew there was a chance, albeit it small, that it might cause an accident?'

In other words, we sometimes need to violate our 'desired' human factors principles of happy co-existence between pilot and machine in order to implement alerting systems. While contentious, many cockpit systems are generally considered huge benefits to aviation safety. However, the capacity for pilots to deal with human-factors shortcomings may be limited while the number of alerting systems in growing, suggesting that their use may need to be carefully metered within the cockpit, and carefully delimited from mundane presentations of status. We may be reaching limits on the safety improvements achievable by adding more alerting systems to the cockpit.

---

[2] American news programme which has debated the implementation of safety systems such as automotive airbags.

However, there is much more insight that the human factors community can bring to the design and implementation of alerting systems. In 1980, Wiener and Curry suggested important questions about alerting systems. The answers to some of these are starting to be known: Why can alarms go unheeded? Why can a false alarm rate be so high? Is there a need for a preview alert? Others are now become more pressing: Will/should the operators check the alarm? Will the alerting logic be too complex, especially in the case of prioritised alerts, for operators to perform validity checks and thus lead to over-reliance on the system? Will the system always be correct, and if not, will the operators recognise this?

Many aspects of these unanswered questions revolve around the role of the alerting system vis-à-vis the pilot. The bulk of human factors knowledge about pilot interaction with alerting systems covers primarily the attention-director role. Modern alerting systems are capable of many other roles, some of which are not always recognised during design and testing. As such, study is also required into the human factors issues with these roles, singly and collectively, and their impact on pilots in both normal operations and once an alert has been triggered.

As alerting systems become more capable, some of these human factors issues can become quite fundamental. Who's in charge? Is the entity with the responsibility also given the capacity to make a substantiated decision? These are not new questions; concerns raised at a 1963 autoland conference mirror current issues with alerting systems:

'A conclusion seems to follow from the above comments. If a suitable means is not provided to the pilot to enable him to land the airplane, then a suitable means should be provided to prevent the pilot from interfering with the automation during the last critical phase... It follows therefore that, if the full authority is left to the pilot, the actual reliability level is just that of the pilot himself with the information he has got, irrespective of the possible much higher reliability level of the black boxes – and the aircraft.' (Bartoli, 1963).

'[We] have been striving ... [to] retain the preponderance of the control in the hands of the captain and his crew not only in favor of their dignity but also in favor of overall safety... We would like to see the Autoland used as the autopilot is used during cruise, that is to say as an aid and a contribution to rest rather than a new pain in the neck.' (Turcat, 1963).

For systems where the desired role is to have the pilot actively involved in the control loop, the aviation community still has several large issues to solve. Mosier (1996) pointed out common myths in the use of automation, including that the operator can't disregard an authoritative and knowledgeable system, and that he or she can't always recognise when such a system is making a mistake. Eliminating these myths as design assumptions, and creating automation designs that prevent their associated problems, in practice, is at this time a fledgling endeavour compared to the volume of new technologies under development. Most alerting systems additionally must face these issues in the face of rare, hazardous, time-critical events, and often rely primarily on pilot trust in the alerting system.

For systems where it is not desired to have the pilot cognitively involved in diagnosis and resolution, the issue to be addressed is whether the pilot should be in the control loop at all. Bainbridge (1983) noted the tendency to automate the operator out of the system – in this case the issue is automating the operator into the system. Without cognitive involvement, he or she is reduced to the level of an actuator with notoriously poor reaction time and accuracy. Rather than presenting the illusion that the pilot is in charge of a situation, it may be best to remove him or her from the control loop altogether, and place the burden of proof on the automated system's designer that it has the same performance, in the full range of operational contexts, as is normally expected from the pilot. Until such a design is demonstrated, every effort is required to keep the pilot cognitively involved in resolving critical hazards.

References

Bainbridge, L. (1983). Ironies of automation. *Automatica, 19,* 775-779.

Bartoli, G. (1963). Pilot and reliability. *5th technical conference on all-weather landing and take-off.* Lucerne.

Bilimoria, K.D. (1998). A methodology for the performance evaluation of a conflict probe. *Proceedings of the AIAA guidance, navigation and control conference.* Reston, VA: American Institute of Aeronautics and Astronautics.

Billings, C.E. (1997). *Aviation automation: the search for a human-centered approach.* Mahwah, NJ: Lawrence Erlbaum.

Bliss, J.P., Gilson, R.D. and Deaton, J.E. (1995). Human probability matching behaviour in response to alarms of varying reliability. *Ergonomics, 38,* 2300-2312.

Bliss, J.P., Jeans, S.M. and Prioux, H.J. (1996). Dual-task performance as a function of individual alarm validity and alarm system reliability information. *Proceedings of the human factors and ergonomics society, 40th annual meeting.* Santa Monica, CA: Human Factors and Ergonomics Society.

Block, F.E., Nuutinen, L. and Ballast, B., (1999). Optimization of alarms: a study on alarm limits, alarm sounds and false alarms, intended to reduce annoyance. *Journal of clinical monitoring and computing, 15,* 75-83.

Borndorff-Eccarius, S. and Johannsen, G. (1993). Supporting diagnostic functions in human supervisory control. *Proceedings of the IEEE international conference on systems, man and cybernetics* (pp. 351-356). Piscataway, NJ: IEEE.

Cooper, G.E. (1977). *A survey of the status and philosophies relating to cockpit warning systems* (NASA Contractor Report CR-152071). Moffett Field, CA: NASA Ames Research Center.

Davis, S.D. and Pritchett, A.R. (1999). Alerting system assertiveness, knowledge, and over-reliance. *Journal of information technology impact, 3,* 119-143.

Dingus, T.A., McGehee, D.V., Manakkal, N., Jahns, S.K., Carney, C. and Hankey, J.M. (1997). Human factors field evaluation of automotive headway maintenance/ collision warning devices. *Human factors, 39*, 216-229.

Elvers, G.C. and Elrif, P. (1997). The effects of correlation and response bias in alerted monitor displays. *Human factors, 39*, 570-580.

Endsley, M. (1995). Toward a theory of situation awareness in dynamic systems. *Human factors special issue: Situation awareness, 37*, 32-64.

Faitakis, Y.E., Thapliyal, S. and Kantor, J.C. (1998). An LMI approach to the evaluation of alarm thresholds. *International journal of robust and nonlinear control, 8*, 659-667.

Flight Safety Foundation (1997). *Controlled flight into terrain: education and training aid*. Arlington, VA: Flight Safety Foundation.

Getty, D.J., Swets, J.A. and Pickett, R.M. (1994). *The pilot's response to warnings: a laboratory investigation of the effects on human response time of the costs and benefits of responding* (Report No. 7947). Cambridge MA: BBN Systems and Technologies.

Guerlain, S.A., Smith, P.J., Obradovich, J.H., Rudmann, S., Strohm, P., Smith, J.W., Svirbely, J. and Sachs, L. (1999). Interactive critiquing as a form of decision support: An empirical evaluation. *Human factors, 41*, 72-89.

Hasse, D. (1992). ALPA ground proximity warning system survey. *Proceedings of the flight safety foundation 45th annual international air safety seminar* (pp. 38-44). Arlington, VA: Flight Safety Foundation.

Heimdahl, M., Leveson, N.G. and Reese, J.D. (1998). Experiences from specifying the TCAS II requirements using RSML. *Proceedings of the 1998 17th AIAA/IEEE/SAE digital avionics systems conference*, (Volume 1, pp. C43-1 to C43-8). Piscataway, NJ: IEEE.

Hickling, E.M. (1994). Modern nuclear power plants: alarm system design. In N. Stanton (Ed.) *Human factors in alarm design* (pp. 165-178). London: Taylor and Francis.

Horn, J. (1999). *Flight envelope limit detection and avoidance*. Unpublished doctoral dissertation, Georgia Institute of Technology, Atlanta.

Kantowitz, B.H. and Casper, P.A. (1988). Human workload in aviation. In E.L. Wiener and D.C. Nagel (Eds.) *Human factors in aviation* (pp. 157-188). San Diego, CA: Academic Press.

Kerstholt, J.H., Passenier, P.O., Houttuin, K. and Schuffel, H. (1996). The effect of a priori probability and complexity on decision making in a supervisory control task. *Human factors, 38*, 65-78.

Kirlik, A (1993). Modeling strategic behavior in human-automation interaction: why an 'aid' can (and should) go unused. *Human factors, 35*, 221-242.

Klass, P.J. (1998, April 27). Eurocontrol mandates TCAS / 7.0 software installation. *Aviation week and space technology*, pp. 51-52.

Kuchar, J.K (1996). Methodology for alerting-system performance evaluation. *Journal of guidance, control and dynamics, 19*, 438-444.

Kuchar, J.K. and Carpenter, B.D. (1997). Airborne collision alerting logic for closely-spaced parallel approach. *Air traffic control quarterly, 5*, 1997.

Lee, J. and Moray, N. (1992). Trust, control strategies and allocation of function in human-machine systems. *Ergonomics, 35*, 1243-1270.

Lee, J. and Moray, N. (1994). Trust, self-confidence, and operator's adaptation to automation. *International journal of human-computer studies, 40*, 153-184.

Liu, H.T., Golborne, C., Bun, Y. and Martel, M. (1998). Surface windshear alert system, part 1: prototype development. *Journal of aircraft, 35*, 422-428.

Marshall, E. and Baker, S. (1994). Alarms in nuclear power plant control rooms. In N. Stanton (Ed.) *Human factors in alarm design* (pp. 183-191). London: Taylor and Francis.

Mårtensson, L. (1995). The aircraft crash at Gottröra: experiences of the cockpit crew. *International journal of aviation psychology, 5*, 305-326.

Mellone, V.J. (1993, June). Genie out of the bottle? *ASRS directline*, Issue No. 4.

Meredith, C. and Edworthy, J. (1994). Sources of confusion in intensive therapy unit alarms. In N. Stanton (Ed.) *Human factors in alarm design* (pp. 207-219). London: Taylor and Francis.

Midkiff and Hansman (1993). Identification of important 'party line' information elements and implications for situational awareness in the datalink environment. *Air traffic control quarterly, 1*, 5-30.

Molloy, R. and Parasuraman, R. (1996). Monitoring an automated system for a single failure: vigilance and task complexity effects. *Human factors, 38*, 311-322.

Mosier, K.L. (1996). Myths of expert decision making and automated decision aids. In C.E. Zsambok and G. Klein (Eds.) *Naturalistic decision making* (pp. 319-330). Mahwah, NJ: Lawrence Erlbaum.

Mosier, K.L and Skitka, L.J. (1996). Human decision makers and automated decision aids: made for each other? In, R. Parasuraman and M. Mouloua (Eds.) *Automation and human performance: theory and applications* (pp. 201-220). Mahwah NJ: Lawrence Erlbaum.

Muir, B.M. (1987). Trust between humans and machines, and the design of decision aids. *International journal of man-machine studies, 27*, 527-539.

Muir, B.M. (1994). Trust in automation: I. Theoretical issues in the study of trust and human intervention in automated systems. *Ergonomics special issue: Cognitive ergonomics, 37*, 1905-1922.

Noyes, J.M, Cresswell-Starr, A.F. and Rankin, J.A. (1999). Designing aircraft warning systems: a case study. In, N.A. Stanton and J. Edworthy (Eds.), *Human factors in auditory warnings* (pp. 265-281). Aldershot, England: Ashgate.

Noyes, J.M. and Starr, A.F. (2000). Civil aircraft warning systems: future directions in information management and presentation. *International journal of aviation psychology, 10*, 169-188.

Parasuraman, R., Hancock, P.A. and Olofinboba, O. (1997). Alarm effectiveness in driver-centered collision-warning systems. *Ergonomics, 40*, 390-399.

Parasuraman, R., Molloy, R., Mouloua, M. and Hilburn, B. (1996) Monitoring of automated systems. In, R. Parasuraman and M. Mouloua (Eds.) *Automation and human performance: theory and applications* (pp. 91-115). Mahwah NJ: Lawrence Erlbaum.

Parasurman, R. and Riley, V. (1997). Humans and automation: use, misuse, disuse, abuse. *Human factors, 39*, 230-253.

Paté-Cornell, M.E. (1986). Warning systems in risk management. *Risk analysis, 6*, 223-234.

Pritchett, A.R., Vándor, B. and Edwards, K.E. (1999, June). Testing and implementing cockpit alerting systems. Presented at *Human error, safety, and system development*, Liége, Belgium.

Proctor, P. (1998, April 6). Integrated cockpit safety system certified. *Aviation week and space technology*, p. 61.

Riley, V. (1996). Operator reliance on automation: theory and data. In R. Parasuraman and M. Mouloua (Eds.) *Automation and human performance: theory and applications* (pp. 19-35). Mahwah NJ: Lawrence Erlbaum.

Riley, V., DeMers, R., Good, M., Krishnan, K., Miller, C. and Misiak, C. (1996). *Crew-centered flight deck alerting*. Minneapolis, MN: Honeywell Technical Center.

Rogers, W.H., Schutte, P.C. and Latorella, K.A. (1996). Fault management in aviation systems. In, R. Parasuraman and M. Mouloua (Eds.) *Automation and human performance: theory and applications* (pp. 281-317). Mahwah NJ: Lawrence Erlbaum.

Rouse, W.B. (1983). Models of human problem solving: detection, diagnosis and compensation for system failures. *Automatica, 19*, 613-625.

Radio Technical Commission for Aeronautics (RTCA) (1983). *Minimum operational performance standards for traffic alert and collision avoidance system (TCAS) airborne equipment* (RTCA / DO – 185). Washington, DC: RTCA.

Sarter, N.B. and Woods, D.D. (1992). Pilot interaction with cockpit automation: operational experiences with the flight management system. *International journal of aviation psychology, 2*, 303-321.

Sarter, N.B. and Woods, D.D. (1994). Pilot interaction with cockpit automation II: an experimental study of pilots' model and awareness of the flight management system. *International journal of aviation psychology, 4*, 1-28.

Scott, W.B. (1999, February 1). Automatic GCAS: 'you can't fly any lower'. *Aviation week and space technology*, pp. 76-80.

See, J.E., Warm, J.S., Dember, W.N. and Howe, S.R. (1997). Vigilance and signal detection theory: an empirical evaluation of five measures of response bias. *Human factors, 39*, 14-29.

Sheridan, T.B. (1992). *Telerobotics, automation and human supervisory control*. Cambridge, MA: MIT Press.

Sklar, A.E. and Sarter, N.B (2000). Good vibrations: tactile feedback in support of attention allocation and human-automation coordination in event-driven domains. *Human factors, 41*, 543-552.

Sorkin, R.D., Kantowitz, B.H. and Kantowitz, S.C. (1988). Likelihood alarm displays. *Human factors, 30*, 445-459.

Sorkin, R.D. and Woods, D.D. (1985). Systems with human monitors: a signal detection analysis. *Human-computer interaction, 1*, 49-75.

Stanton, N.A. and Baber, C. (1995). Alarm-initiated activities: An analysis of alarm handling by operators using text-based alarm systems in supervisory control systems. *Ergonomics special issue: Warnings in research and practice, 38*, 2414-2431.

Stanton, N.A. and Edworthy, J. (Eds.). (1999). *Human factors in auditory warnings*. Aldershot, England: Ashgate.

Trujillo, A.C. (1996, February).*Airline transport pilot preferences for predictive information*. NASA Technical Memorandum (NASA TM 4702). Hampton, VA: NASA Langley Research Center.

Turcat, A. (1963). The pilot and the all-weather landing. *5th technical conference on all-weather landing and take-off*. Lucerne.

United Airlines (1998). *B-777 Flight Manual*.

Vallauri, E. (1995). *Operational evaluation of TCAS II in France* (CENA/ R95-04). Toulouse: Centre D'Études de la Navigation Aérienne.

Vallauri, E. (1997). *Suivi de la mise en oeuvre du TCAS II en France en 1996* [1996 Survey of TCAS II implementation in France] (CENA/ R97-16). Toulouse: Centre D'Études de la Navigation Aérienne.

Vándor, B. and Pritchett, A.R. (1999, January). *Effects of displays and alerts on subject reactions to potential collisions during closely spaced parallel approaches* (ISyE Report R-99-02). Atlanta GA: Georgia Institute of Technology.

Veitengruber, J.E. (1977). Design criteria for aircraft warning, caution, and advisory alerting systems. *Journal of aircraft, 15*, 574-581.

Wiener, E.L. (1989). *Human factors of advanced technology ('glass cockpit') transport aircraft* (NASA Technical Report 117528). Moffett Field, CA: NASA Ames research center.

Wiener, E.L. and Curry, R.E. (1980). Flight-deck automation: Promises and problems. *Ergonomics, 23*, 995-1011.

Williamson, T. and Spencer, N.A. (1989). Development and operation of the traffic alert and collision avoidance system (TCAS). *Proceedings of the IEEE, 77*, 1735-1744.

Winder, L.F. and Kuchar, J.K. (2000). *Generalized philosophy of alerting with applications for parallel approach collision prevention* (ICAT Report ICAT-2000-5). Cambridge MA: Massachusetts Institute of Technology.

Woods, D.D. (1986). Paradigms for decision support. In, E. Hollnagel (Ed.), *Intelligent decision support in process environments* (NATA ASI Series, Vol. F21, 153-173). Heidelberg: Springer-Verlag.

Woods, D.D. (1995). The alarm problem and directed attention in dynamic fault management. *Ergonomics, 38*, 2371-2393.

Yang, L.C. and Kuchar, J.K. (1997). Prototype conflict alerting logic for free flight. *Journal of guidance, control and dynamics, 20*, 768-773.

FORMAL PAPERS

The disembodiment of data in the analysis of human factors accidents

Sidney W. A. Dekker
Centre for Human Factors in Aviation, IKP
Linköping Institute of Technology, Sweden

Abstract

This article examines the theoretical underpinnings of human factors investigations in aviation. Many investigations today disembody their human factors data, either through micro-matching (behavioural fragments with after-the-fact worlds) or cherry-picking (fragments that seem to point to a common psychological condition). The reasons and mechanisms of disembodiment stem in part from conventional and technological restrictions on the gathering and analysis of human factors data. But they also have to do with our reactions to failure, which easily make investigations retrospective, proximal, counterfactual and judgmental. In addition, methodical guidance on how to map context-specific details of a complex behavioural sequence onto a conceptual description is hardly available. Instead, investigators typically rely on inarticulate folk models that make broad, unverifiable psychological assertions about the observed particulars. This article presents possible progress in the form of steps investigators can take to reconstruct the unfolding mindset of the people they are investigating, in parallel and tight connection with how the world was evolving around these people at the time.

Correspondence: Sidney W. A. Dekker, Centre for Human Factors in Aviation, IKP, Linköping Institute of Technology, SE – 581 83, Linköping, SWEDEN or sidde@ikp.liu.se

Introduction

Developments in digital and other recording technologies have enlarged our ability to capture human performance data—in aviation as well as other industries where people interact with technology in complex, dynamic environments. In commercial aviation, the electronic footprint that any incident or accident leaves can be huge. Recent initiatives such as the formation of a Future Flight Data Committee in the US, and regulatory proposals to lengthen recording times on cockpit voice recorders (Flight International, 1999) testify to the value we attach to accessible chronicles of human behaviour (e.g. Baker, 1999). But capturing human factors data addresses only one side of the problem. Our ability to make sense of these data, to reconstruct how humans contributed to an unfolding sequence of events, may not have kept pace with our growing technical ability to register traces of their behaviour. In other words, the growing dominance of human factors in incidents and accidents (Boeing, 1994) is not matched by our ability to analyse or understand the human contribution for what it is worth (McIntyre, 1994).

Data used in human factors accident analysis often comes from a recording of human voices and perhaps other sounds (ruffling charts, turning knobs), which can be coupled to a greater or lesser extent to contemporaneous system or process behaviour. A voice trace, however, represents only a partial data record. Human behaviour in rich, unfolding settings is much more than the voice trace it leaves behind. The voice trace always points beyond itself, to a world that was unfolding around the practitioners at the time, to tasks, goals, perceptions, intentions, thoughts and actions that have since evaporated. But aircraft accident investigations are formally restricted in how they can couple the cockpit voice recording to the world that was unfolding around the practitioners (e.g. instrument indications, automation mode settings). ICAO Annex 13 prescribes how only those data that can be factually established may be analysed in the search for cause. This provision often leaves the cockpit voice recording as only factual, decontextualized and impoverished footprint of human performance. Making connections between the voice trace and the circumstances and people in which it was grounded quickly falls outside the pale of official analysis and into the realm of what many would call inference or speculation.

Apart from the provisions of Annex 13, this problem is complicated by the fact that current flight data recorders often do not capture many automation-related traces: precisely those data that are of immediate importance to understanding the problem-solving environment in which most pilots today carry out their work. For example, FDR's in many highly automated aircraft do not record which ground-based navigation beacons were selected by the pilots, what automation mode control panel selections on airspeed, heading, altitude and vertical speed were made, or what was shown on the both pilots' moving map displays. As pilot work has shifted to the management and supervision of a suite of automated resources (Billings, 1997; Dekker and Hollnagel, 1999), and problems leading to accidents increasingly start in human-machine interactions, this represents a large gap in our ability to access the reasons for particular human assessments and actions in cockpits.

Situated cognition—but decontextualized investigations

The inability to make clear connections between behaviour and world straightjackets any study of the human contribution to a cognitively noisy, evolving sequence of events. Basic findings from cognitive science and related fields keep stressing how human performance is fundamentally embedded in, and systematically connected to, the situation in which it takes place (Neisser, 1976; Gibson, 1979; Winograd and Flores, 1987; Varela *et al.*, 1995; Clark, 1997). Human actions and assessments can be described meaningfully only in reference to the world in which they are made (Winograd, 1987; Suchman, 1987); they cannot be understood without intimately linking them to details of the context that produced and accompanied them (Orasanu and Connolly, 1993; Woods *et al.*, 1994; Hutchins, 1995; Klein, 1998).

Despite this balance of scientific opinion (e.g. Willems and Raush, 1969), critical voice traces from aircraft mishaps are basically left to be examined outside the context that produced them; and outside the context in which they once carried meaning. As a result, investigators easily confuse their own reality with the one that surrounded the practitioners in question. There appear to be two broad patterns in this confusion—two ways in which human factors data are taken out of context and given meaning in relation to after-the-fact worlds. The section that follows discusses these two patterns of disembodiment. The remainder of the article explores the reasons and mechanisms behind the disembodiment of data, including retrospection and the social construction of cause, and human factors' susceptibility to folk modelling. The article then points to opportunities for progress.

Two forms of disembodiment: Micro-matching and cherry picking

Micro-matching: holding individual performance fragments against the background of a world we now know to be true

Faced with complex and temporally extended behavioural situations, a dominant tactic people use is to restrict the situation under consideration by concentrating on only one isolated fragment at a time (Woods, 1993). Thus, an incident or accident sequence is typically parsed up into individual controversial decision points that can then be scrutinised for accuracy or reasonableness in isolation. This can for example be the 'decision' of a crew to continue their approach into conditions investigators now know produced a microburst (NTSB, 1995). Rather than understanding these controversial fragments in relation to the circumstances that brought them forth, and in relation to the stream of preceding as well as succeeding behaviours which surrounded them, the performance fragment is held up against a world investigators now know to be true. The problem is this after-the-fact-world may have very little relevance to the actual world that produced the behaviour under investigation. The behaviour is contrasted against the investigator's reality, not the reality surrounding the behaviour in question. There are various ways in which such after-the-fact-worlds can be brought into being; three are mentioned here.

First, individual fragments of behaviour are frequently contrasted with written guidance, which can be found to have been applicable in hindsight. Compared with such written guidance, actual performance is often found wanting; it does not live up to procedures or regulations. For example, 'One of the pilots...executed (a computer entry) without having verified that it was the correct selection and without having first obtained approval of the other pilot, contrary to AA's procedures.' Investigations invest considerably in organisational archaeology so that they can construct the regulatory or procedural framework within which the operations took place. Inconsistencies between existing procedures or regulations and actual behaviour are easy to expose when organisational records are excavated after-the-fact and rules uncovered that would have fit this or that particular situation. This is not, however, very informative. There is virtually always a mismatch between actual behaviour and written guidance that can be located in hindsight (Suchman, 1987; Woods *et al.*, 1994). Pointing that there is a mismatch sheds little light on the *why* of the behaviour in question. And for that matter, mismatches between procedures and practice are not unique to mishaps (Degani and Wiener, 1991).

Second, to construct the world against which investigators hold individual performance fragments, can exist of elements in the situation that were not picked up by the practitioners (Endsley, 1999), but that, in hindsight, proved critical. Take the turn towards the mountains on the left that was made just before an accident near Cali, Colombia in 1995 (Aeronautica Civil, 1996). What should the crew have seen in order to notice the turn? They had plenty of indications, according to the manufacturer of their aircraft:

'Indications that the airplane was in a left turn would have included the following: the EHSI (Electronic Horizontal Situation Indicator) Map Display (if selected) with a curved path leading away from the intended direction of flight; the EHSI VOR display, with the CDI (Course Deviation Indicator) displaced to the right, indicating the airplane was left of the direct Cali VOR course, the EaDI indicating approximately 16 degrees of bank, and all heading indicators moving to the right. Additionally the crew may have tuned Rozo in the ADF and may have had bearing pointer information to Rozo NDB on the RMDI' (Boeing, 1996, p. 13).

This is a standard response after mishaps: point to the data that would have revealed the true nature of the situation (Woods, 1995). Knowledge of the 'critical' data comes only with the omniscience of hindsight, but if data can be shown to have been physically available, it is assumed that it should have been picked up by the practitioners in the situation. The problem is that pointing out that it should have does not explain why it was not, or why it was interpreted differently back then (Weick, 1995). There is a dissociation between data availability and data observability (Woods, 1995)—between what can be shown to have been physically available and what would have been observable given the multiple interleaving tasks, goals, attentional focus, interests, and—as Vaughan (1996) shows—culture of the practitioner.

Third, there are less obvious or documented standards. These are often invoked when a controversial fragment (e.g. a decision to accept a runway change (Aeronautica Civil, 1996; or the decision to go around or not, NTSB, 1995) knows no clear pre-ordained guidance but relies on local, situated judgement. For these cases there are always 'standards of good practice' which are based on convention and putatively practised across an entire industry. One such standard in aviation is 'good airmanship', which, if nothing else can, will explain the variance in behaviour that had not yet been accounted for.

Investigators micro-match controversial fragments of behaviour with standards that seem applicable from their after-the-fact position. The problem is that these after-the-fact-worlds may have very little relevance to the circumstances of the accident sequence, and that the investigator has substituted his own world for the one that surrounded the practitioners in question.

Cherry picking: grouping similar performance fragments under a label identified in hindsight

Grouping individual fragments of human performance that *prima facie* represent some common condition, is the second pattern in which meaning is imposed on available data from the outside and from hindsight. Consider the following example, where diverse fragments of performance—that are not temporally co-located but spread out over half an hour—are lumped together to build a case for haste as explanation of the (in hindsight) bad decisions taken by the crew:

'Investigators were able to identify a series of errors that initiated with the flightcrew's acceptance of the controller's offer to land on runway 19...The CVR indicates that the decision to accept the offer to land on runway 19 was made jointly by the captain and the first officer in a 4-second exchange that began at 2136:38. The captain asked: 'would you like to shoot the one nine straight in?' The first officer responded, 'Yeah, we'll have to scramble to get down. We can do it.' This interchange followed an earlier discussion in which the captain indicated to the first officer his desire to hurry the arrival into Cali, following the delay on departure from Miami, in an apparent to minimise the effect of the delay on the flight attendants' rest requirements. For example, at 2126:01, he asked the first officer to 'keep the speed up in the descent'... The evidence of the hurried nature of the tasks performed and the inadequate review of critical information between the time of the flightcrew's acceptance of the offer to land on runway 19 and the flight's crossing the initial approach fix, ULQ, indicates that insufficient time was available to fully or effectively carry out these actions. Consequently, several necessary steps were performed improperly or not at all' (Aeronautica Civil, 1996, p. 29).

It is easy to pick through the voice record of an accident sequence and find fragments that all seem to point to a common condition. The investigator treats the voice record as if it were a public quarry to select stones from, and the accident explanation the building he needs to erect. The problem is that each fragment is meaningless outside the context that produced it: each fragment has its own story, background, and reasons for being, and when it was produced it may have had nothing to do with the other fragments it is now grouped with. Also, behaviour takes place in between the fragments. These intermediary episodes contain changes and evolutions in perceptions and assessments that separate the excised fragments not only in time, but also in meaning.

Thus, the condition that binds *prima facie* similar performance fragments arises not from the circumstances that brought each of the fragments forth; it is not a feature of those circumstances. It is an artefact of the investigator. In the case described above, 'hurry' is a condition identified in hindsight, one that plausibly couples the start of the flight (almost 2 hours behind schedule) with its fatal ending (on a mountainside rather than an airport). 'Hurry' is a retrospectively invoked *leitmotif* that guides the search for evidence about itself. This leaves an investigation not with findings, but with tautologies.

Investigations as social reconstructions

Retrospective

Investigations aim to explain the past. Yet they are conducted in the present, and thus inevitably influenced by it. One safe bet is that investigators know more about the mishap than the people who were caught up in it. Investigators and other retrospective observers know the true nature of the situation surrounding the people at the time (where they were versus where they thought they were, what mode their system was in versus what mode they thought it was in, and so forth). Investigators also know the outcome and inevitably evaluate people's assessments and actions in the light of it. The effects of this hindsight bias have been well-documented and even reproduced under controlled circumstances (Fischoff, 1975). One effect is that 'people who know the outcome of a complex prior history of tangled, indeterminate events remember that history as being much more determinant, leading 'inevitably' to the outcome they already knew' (Weick, 1995, p28). Hindsight allows us to change past indeterminacy and complexity into order, structure, and oversimplified causality (Reason, 1990). The problem is that structure is itself an artefact of hindsight—only hindsight can turn ill-structured, confusing and blurred events into clear decision paths with junctures which shows where practitioners went the wrong way. Second, to explain failure, we seek failure. We seek the incorrect actions, the flawed analyses, and the inaccurate perceptions, even if these were not thought to be influential or obvious at the time (Starbuck and Milliken, 1988). This search for people's failures is the result of the hindsight bias: knowledge of outcome influences how we see a process. If we know the outcome was bad, we can no longer objectively look at the behaviour leading up to it—it must also have been bad (Fischoff, 1975; Woods *et al.*, 1994).

Proximal, counterfactual and judgmental

It is not just knowledge of outcome and wider circumstance that colours the interpretation of past behavioural data. Investigations are governed by implicit goals that go beyond merely 'understanding' what went wrong and preventing recurrence. Mishaps are surprising relative to prevailing beliefs and assumptions about the system in which they happen (Wagenaar and Groeneweg, 1987). Thus, investigations are inevitably affected by the concern to reconcile a disruptive event with existing views and beliefs about the system. In this process of reconciliation, something has to give—either the event, or the existing beliefs about the system.

In the immediate aftermath of failure, people and institutions may be willing to question their underlying assumptions about the system they use or operate. Perhaps things are not as safe as previously thought; perhaps the system contains error-producing conditions that could have spawned this kind of failure earlier, or worse, could do it again. This openness does not typically last long. As the shock of an accident subsides, parts of the system mobilise to contain systemic self-doubt and change the fundamental surprise into a merely local hick-up that temporarily ruffled an otherwise smooth operation. The reassurance is that the system is basically safe—it's only some people or other parts in it that are unreliable. In the end, it is not often that an existing view of a system gives in to the reality of failure. Instead the event, or the players in it, are changed to fit existing assumptions and beliefs about the system, rather than the other way around. Expensive lessons about the system as a whole, and the subtle vulnerabilities it contains, can go completely unlearned (e.g. Rasmussen and Batstone, 1989; Wilkinson, 1994).

Human factors investigations must be understood against the backdrop of the 'fundamental surprise error' (Lanir, 1986) and examined for the role they play in it. The inability to deal with the fundamental surprise of a failure shines through investigations that are:

- proximal: they concentrate on local perpetrators: those closest to 'causing' and potentially preventing the failure are seen as the sole engine of action;
- counterfactual: they state what these practitioners could have done to prevent the outcome;
- judgmental: they state how practitioners 'failed' to take these actions or notice data that they should have noticed.

An investigation's emphasis on the proximal ensures that the mishap remains the result of a few uncharacteristically ill-performing individuals who are not representative of the system or the larger practitioner population in it. It leaves existing beliefs about the basic safety of the system intact.

The pilots of a large military helicopter that crashed on a hillside in Scotland in 1994 were found guilty of gross negligence. The pilots did not survive—29 people died in total—so their side of the story could never be heard. The official inquiry had no problems with 'destroying the reputation of two good men', as a fellow pilot put it. Potentially fundamental vulnerabilities (such as 160 reported cases of Uncommanded Flying Control Movement or UFCM in computerised helicopters alone since 1994) were not looked into seriously (Sunday Times, 25 June 2000).

Counterfactuals enumerate the possible pathways that practitioners could have taken to prevent the mishap (the pathways that look so obvious in hindsight). For example:

'... the airplane could have overcome the windshear encounter if the pitch attitude of 15 degrees nose-up had been maintained, the thrust had been set to 1.93, and the landing gear had been retraced on schedule' (NTSB, 1995, p. 119).

Much investigative energy is invested in proving what could have happened if certain minute or utopian conditions had been met, and the result of these efforts is often accepted as explanatory substitute. Counterfactuals may be fruitful in exploring potential countermeasures against the same kind of failure. But counterfactuals explain nothing. Laying out what did not happen does not explain what happened. Counterfactuals also have no empirical justification, as there are no events in the world that beg their kind of illumination.

The step from counterfactual to judgement is a small one, and often taken by investigations. Judgements occur when counterfactual pathways are held up as the ones that *should* have been taken, and they slip into investigations surprisingly easily. Take as an example the probable causes of the previously alluded 1994 aircraft accident at Charlotte, N.C. Among the probable causes were '(2) the flightcrew's failure to recognize a windshear situation in a timely manner; (3) the flightcrew's failure to establish and maintain the proper airplane attitude and thrust setting necessary to escape from windshear' (NTSB, 1995, p. 120). Instead of explaining events from the point of view of the pilots inside of them, the investigation lays out counterfactual pathways and stresses that they should have been taken—which is obvious from hindsight—by asserting that not doing so constituted a failure. None of this explains the practitioners' actual behaviour.

Counterfactual and judgmental language, typical of aircraft accident investigations, justify their proximal emphasis. If only these people had done something different (which was so obvious! How could they have missed it!), then the accident would not have happened. The reason for failure has been located. It truncates the need for deeper probing into the systemic conditions that perhaps laid the groundwork for controversial proximal assessments and actions in the first place.

The social construction of cause

The fundamental surprise error means that events get picked apart and re-inscribed to fit existing assumptions about the system in which it happened, rather than the other way around. Investigations contribute to the error through the disembodiment of data, their proximal focus and counterfactual and judgmental language. As a result, different and mutually exclusive accident investigations can emerge that each emphasise and rely on their own sets of 'cherries' from a single sequence of events (see table 1 for an example)—leaving the larger system or industry none the wiser.

Table 1 Different statements of cause about the same accident. Compiled from Aeronautica Civil (1996) and Flight Safety Foundation (1997).

The Colombian authorities say:	The airline says:
The Cali approach controller did not contribute to the cause of the accident	Approach control clearances were not in accordance with ICAO standards The approach controller's inadequate English and inattention during a critical phase of the approach were causal
... and among the causes are:	... and among the causes are:
Inadequate use of automation	Inadequate navigational database
The lack of pilot situation awareness regarding terrain and navigation aids	Lack of radar coverage over Cali
Failure to revert to radio navigation when FMS created confusion and workload	Manufacturer's/vendor's over-confidence in FMS technology and resultant influence passed onto pilots regarding FMS capabilities
The flight crew's failure to adequately plan and execute the approach to runway 19	Failure of those responsible to ensure that FMS database matched industry advisory
Ongoing efforts to expedite the approach to avoid delays	The crew's task overload caused by unexpected change in assigned runway

The reason that investigations have so many causes to choose from is that the systems that are vulnerable to failure are so well-protected against it. A lot needs to go wrong for a system to be pushed over the edge of breakdown (e.g. Reason, 1997). When tracing a failure chain, causal webs quickly spread out, like cracks in a window. The pattern of contributions to any complex system failure is dense, and 'primary' or 'root' causes that are found in it are arbitrary choices or constructs by the one doing the looking. The example, above shows that the selection or construction of cause is determined in large part by organisational or sociological factors that lie outside the actual events. It also shows that accuracy or comprehensiveness are not criteria for a successful explanation, but plausibility is—plausibility from the point of view of those who have to accommodate the surprise that the failure represents for *them* and *their* organisation. Accident investigations have this purpose to fulfil, even if they become selective oversimplifications because of it. Even if—in the words of Weick (1995)—they make lousy history.

Folk models

Another reason for the disembodiment of data is the paucity of agreed-upon methods for matching the behavioural particulars of an accident sequence with articulated, theory-driven models of human performance. In this sense, human factors data analysis lags behind the investigation of, say, structural crash evidence where recovered bits and pieces can be contrasted against quantitative models of component performance or tests of identical components under similar circumstances (McIntyre, 1994). Conclusions and causal statements flowing forth from such investigations have a measure of reliability—they could in principle be replicated. In contrast, human factors investigators are left to draw inferences and produce ad-hoc assertions that bear some relationship with an ill-defined psychological or sociological phenomenon. For example:

- 'Deficient situation awareness is evident' (Aeronautica Civil, 1996, p. 34)
- 'The CRM (Crew Resource Management) of the crew was deficient' (Aeronautica Civil, 1996, p. 47)
- There was a 'casual atmosphere' (NTSB, 1994, p. 106)
- 'They had lost situation awareness and effective CRM' (Aeronautica Civil, 1996, p. 48).

Such 'explanations' frequently make it into conclusions and statements of cause. For example, 'Aeronautica Civil determines that the probable causes of this accident were:...(3) the lack of situational awareness of the flightcrew...' (1996, p. 57).

What does not help is that the human performance models investigators use, or have available (e.g. 'loss of situation awareness or loss of CRM') are often theory-begging folk models that do little more than parroting popular contemporary consensus between experts and non-experts on the nature of an everyday phenomenon, for example getting lost or confused (Hollnagel, 1998). In response to the increasing dominance of human factors in accidents over the past decades, investigators (as well as researchers) have introduced, loaned or overgeneralised concepts that try to capture critical features of individual or coordinative crew behaviour (for example workload, complacency, stress, situation awareness). While easily mistaken for deeper insight into human factors issues, these concepts can create more confusion than clarity. A credible and detailed mapping between the context-dependent (and measurable) particulars of an accident sequence and pertinent conceptual models is often lacking. The jump from accident details to conceptual conclusions is typically a single and large one, supported by the kind of cherry-picking described above—which immunises it against critique or verification. This is similar to the issue faced by psychological field studies, where the translation from context to concept needs to go through various steps or levels in order for those without access to the original situation to trace and appreciate the conceptual description (Hollnagel, Pederson and Rasmussen, 1981; Woods, 1993).

The problem is that folk models typically lack the human performance measures or probes that would be necessary to reach down into the context-specific details, because they postulate no underlying psychological theory that could deliver any (Hollnagel, 1998). For example, when one pilot asks the other 'where are we?' (Aeronautica Civil, 1996, p. 33), this may be a clear instance of a loss of situation awareness to a lay observer. But there is nothing inherent to models of situation awareness (e.g. Endsley, 1999) that dictates that this would be so: the model proposes no performance measurement based on an underlying psychological theory, i.e. that asking a question involving direction indicates a loss of situation awareness.

Human factors can offer theory-based, well-articulated conceptual models of human performance. But, similar to the issue that confronts field experimentation (Hoffman and Woods, 2000), problems occur because there is little guidance to help investigators establish the mapping between the particulars of context-bound behaviour in an accident episode on the one hand and models or descriptions of human performance that offer a sufficient level of conceptual detail for those kinds of settings on the other (see Woods, 1993 and Klein, 1998 for some achievement in this respect). The lack of guidance is surprising in an era where human factors are judged to be the dominant contributor to system failure (e.g. NTSB, 1994; Boeing, 1994), yet some progress is being made (see Dekker, in press).

Progress on human factors investigations

How do we prevent the disembodiment of data? In order to understand the actual meaning that data had at the time and place it was produced, investigators need to step into the past themselves (Vaughan, 1996). According to Tuchman (1981): 'Every scripture is entitled to be read in the light of the circumstances that brought it forth. To understand the choices open to people of another time, one must limit oneself to what they knew; see the past in its own clothes, as it were, not in ours' (p. 75). When left in the context that produced and surrounded it, human behaviour is inherently meaningful. The challenge for an investigator is to reconstruct the unfolding situation as it looked to the people whose controversial actions and assessments are under investigation. Taking the perspective of people inside the situation means adopting the local rationality principle: these people were doing reasonable things given their point of view, their available knowledge, their objectives and their limited resources (De Keyser and Woods, 1990; Woods, Johannesen, Cook and Sarter, 1994).

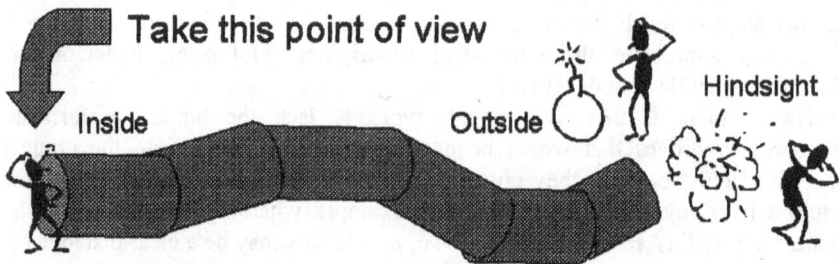

Figure 1 The challenge for an investigator is to reconstruct the situation as it unfolded from the point of view of the people inside of it—free from the biases of the perspective of retrospective outsider.

The local rationality principle implies that investigations should not try to find where people went wrong, but rather understand how people's assessments and actions made sense at the time, given the circumstances that surrounded them.

This requires the investigator to build a picture of:
- how a process and other circumstances unfolded around people;
- how people's assessments and actions evolved in parallel with their changing situation;
- how features of people's tools and tasks and organisational and operational environment influenced their assessments and actions.

In other words, the reconstruction of a practitioner's unfolding mindset begins not with the mind. It begins with the situation in which that mind found itself. Note how this confirms the basic findings about situated cognition: if we understand the circumstances in which human cognition took place, we will begin to understand those cognitive activities. Such reconstruction also diminishes an investigator's dependency on large psychological (folk) labels, instead creating a more direct coupling between (possible) perceptions and actions. Here are some concrete steps that investigators can take (see for more detail: Dekker, in press):

Mark the beginning and end of a sequence of events

This may seem an obvious step to take in any analysis—bound the event under investigation by marking the start and the finish. Yet many investigations do not explicitly say where in a sequence of events their work really begins and where it ends. One reason is the inherent difficulty in deciding what counts as the beginning (especially the beginning—the end of a sequence of events often speaks for itself). But investigations can take as their beginning the first assessment, decision or action by people close to the mishap—the one that, according to the investigator, set the sequence of events in motion. Such a decision may be the pilot's acceptance of a runway change that led to trouble later on. Such a proximal assessment or action can be seen as a trigger for the unfolding events that follow. Of course the trigger itself has reasons, a background, that extends beyond the mishap sequence—both in time and in place. The whole point of taking a proximal assessment or action as starting point is not to ignore these backgrounds, but to identify concrete points to begin an investigation into them.

Lay out the junctures in a sequence of events

This step 'digitises' an analogue history of events to make further analysis possible. In the meandering sequence of events towards an outcome, an investigator can locate junctures ('critical decision points, see Klein, 1998). These are points where for example:
- The sequence of events took a turn towards the outcome.
- The sequence of events momentarily veered away from the outcome.
- The sequence of events could have taken a turn away from the outcome altogether but did not.

What counts as a juncture? As a rule, what people did and what their processes did is tightly interconnected—the two rarely develop independently from one another. Where the process makes its contributions (e.g. an automation mode change) people can get different insights, come to different conclusions or move towards particular decisions. Which in turn may influence how the process is managed. This means that discovering changes in one may lead onto a juncture in the other. Junctures in a sequence of events towards failure can be identified by cross-examining people's decisions, cognitive resets (DeKeyser and Woods, 1990), shifts in behaviour or strategy, actions to influence the process, and changes in the process itself.

Junctures are starting points for investigating the backgrounds, reasons and histories behind them. Where did decisions come from? What pushed them one way rather than the other? In other words, these junctures form the organising thread, for reconstructing the situation that surrounded the people whose assessments and actions are being investigated. Such deeper investigation of a juncture can also make it go away. For example, people seem to decide, in the face of evidence to the contrary, to not change their course of action; to continue with their plan as it is. With hindsight, one may see that people had opportunities to recover from their misunderstanding of the situation, but missed the cues, or misinterpreted them. These 'decisions' to continue, these opportunities to revise, are junctures only in hindsight. To the people caught up in the sequence of events there was not any compelling reason to re-assess their situation or decide against anything. Or else they would have. They were doing what they were doing because they thought they were right; given their understanding of the situation; their pressures.

The challenge becomes to understand how this was not a juncture to the people in question; how their 'decision' to continue was nothing more than continuous behaviour—reinforced by their current understanding of the situation, confirmed by the cues they were focusing on, and reaffirmed by their expectations of how things would develop in the near future.

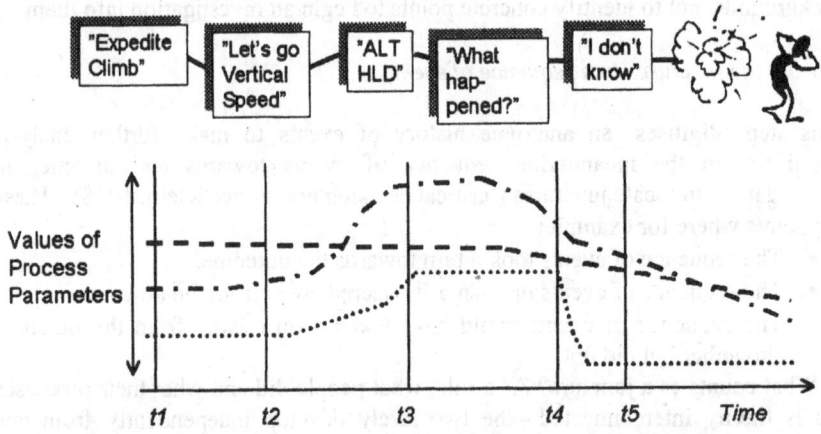

Figure 2 Connecting critical process parameters to the sequence of assessments and actions

Reconstruct the situation at each juncture

How was the world unfolding around people? In an effort to couple cognition to the situation in which it took place, investigators can begin with laying out the critical process parameters and how they were changing over time, both as a result of human influences and of the process moving along. The values of these parameters were likely available to people in all kinds of ways—dials, displays, knobs that pointed certain ways, sounds, mode annunciations, alarms, warnings.

Presenting critical parameters is not new to investigations. Many accident report appendices contain read-outs from data recorders, which show the graphs of known and relevant process parameters. But building these pictures is often where investigations stop today. Tentative references about connections between known parameters and people's assessments and actions are sometimes made, but never in a systematic, or graphic way. The point of step three is to marry all the junctures identified above with the unfolding process—to begin to see the two in parallel, as an inextricable, causal *dance-a-deux*. The point is to build a picture that shows these connections (see figure 2).

As said before, there is a difference between data availability and data observability. Out of the critical parameters what did people actually notice? Where did they look? How did they interpret their evolving situation? The next step can shed some light on this.

Identify tasks and goals

People do not wander through situations aimlessly, simply receiving inputs and producing outcomes as they go along. They are there to get a job done, to accomplish tasks, to pursue goals. If there is anything that determines where people look and how they interpret what they see, it is the goals that they have at the time, and the tasks they are trying to accomplish. Finding what tasks people were working on does not need to be difficult. It often connects directly to how process parameters were unfolding around them.

- What is canonical, or normal at this time in the operation? Tasks relate in systematic ways to stages in a process;
- What was happening in the managed process? Changes here obviously connect to the task people were carrying out;
- What were other people in the operating environment doing? People who work together on common goals often divide the necessary tasks among them in predictable or complementary ways.

Tasks and goals pull red threads through the previously digitised assessments and actions; they connect junctures in coherent and meaningful ways. What people saw or did at any one point is determined in part by past assessments of the situation, and expectations of how it would develop in the future.

Identify other influences on assessments and actions

Human behaviour is determined by many more factors than process parameters. As a rule, however, other influences are less visible and more difficult to recover from the evidence of a mishap. Take organisational pressures to choose schedule over safety, for example. Such pressures exist and exert a powerful influence on the many little local trade-offs people make. Yet especially in the aftermath of failure, these factors easily get rationalised away as being irrelevant or insignificant. As in: real professionals should not be susceptible to those kinds of pressures. Such reactions, however, reveal a profound shortcoming in the understanding of human error. Efforts have been made (e.g. Reason, 1997; Dekker, in press) to direct investigators and managers to those features of an operation and organisation that contribute systematically, but subtly, to the assessments and actions that people make on the line.

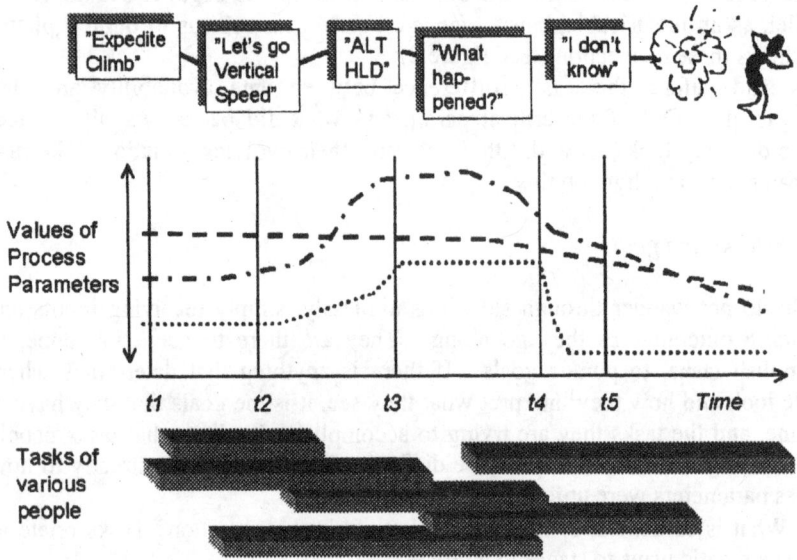

Figure 3 Laying out the tasks that people tried to accomplish during the sequence of events

Conclusion

The treatment and analysis of human factors data in aircraft accident investigations is still a young and somewhat uncertain activity. Micro-matching (fragments of behaviour with after-the-fact worlds) and cherry-picking (fragments that seem to fit a common psychological condition) as investigative practices divorce human factors data from the context in which they were produced. Methodical guidance on how to map context-specific details of a complex behavioural sequence onto a conceptual description instead, is hardly available, and investigators typically rely on inarticulate folk models that make broad, unverifiable psychological assertions about the observed particulars. Also, investigations inevitably have to deal with the surprising nature of failures, easily making them retrospective, proximal, counterfactual and judgmental.

Conventional and technological restrictions also play a role in the disembodiment of data. Further refining of flight recorder parameters, especially on automated flight decks, will help capture those traces necessary to understand the human contribution to most failures today. And a reconsideration of ICAO Annex 13 in light of the increasing popularity of human factors—making that human behaviour and the world in which it was embedded can formally be coupled together during an investigation—is another good start. In the words of McIntyre (1994, p. 18):

'Human factors data should be subject to the same rules of evidence that are applied to other mishap data. Findings must relate to factors which were significant in the mishap scenario and be integrated with other factual evidence.'

References

Aeronautica Civil (1996). *Aircraft accident report: Controlled flight into terrain, American Airlines flight 965, Boeing 757-223, N651AA near Cali, Colombia, December 20, 1995.* Bogota, Colombia: Aeronautica Civil.

Baker, S. (1999). Aviation incident and accident investigation. In, D. J. Garland, J. A. Wise, and V. D. Hopkin (Eds.). *Handbook of aviation human factors*, (pp. 631-642). Mahwah, NJ: Erlbaum.

Billings, C. E. (1997). *Aviation automation: The search for a human-centered approach.* Mahwah, NJ: Erlbaum.

Boeing Commercial Airplane Group (1994). *Statistical summary of commercial jet aircraft accidents: Worldwide operations 1959-1993* (Boeing Airplane Safety Engineering B-210B). Seattle, WA: Boeing.

Boeing Commercial Airplane Group (1996). *Boeing submission to the American Arilines Flight 965 Accident Investigation Board.* Seattle, WA: Boeing.

Clark, A (1997). *Being there: Putting brain, body and world together again.* Cambridge, MA: MIT Press.

Degani, A. and Wiener, E. L. (1991). Philosophy, policies and procedures: The three P's of flightdeck operations. *Paper presented at the Sixth International Symposium on Aviation Psychology, Columbus, OH*, April.

De Keyser, V. and Woods, D. D. (1990). Fixation errors: Failures to revise situation assessment in dynamic and risky systems. In, A. G. Colombo and A. Saiz de Bustamante (Eds.). *System reliability assessment* (pp. 231-251). The Netherlands: Kluwer Academic.

Dekker, S. W. A. (in press). *The field guide to human error.* Bedford, UK: Cranfield University Press.

Dekker, S. W. A. and Hollnagel E. (1999). *Coping with computers in the cockpit.* Aldershot, UK: Ashgate.

Endsley, M. R. (1999). Situation Awareness in aviation systems. In, D. J. Garland, J. A. Wise and V. D. Hopkin (Eds.), *Handbook of aviation human factors* (pp. 257-276). Mahwah, NJ: Erlbaum.

Fischoff, B. (1975). Hindsight is not foresight: The effect of outcome knowledge on judgement under uncertainty. *Journal of Experimental Psychology: Human Perception and Performance, 1,* 288-299.

Flight Safety Foundation (1997). Preparing for a last-minute runway change, Boeing 757 flight crew loses situational awareness, resulting in collision with terrain. *FSF Accident Prevention, July-August* (pp. 1-23). Washington, DC: FSF.

Gibson, J. J. (1979). *The ecological approach to visual perception.* Boston, MA: Houghton-Mifflin.

Hoffman, R. R. and Woods, D. D. (2000). Studying cognitive systems in context. *Human factors, 42,* 1-7.

Hollnagel, E., Pederson, O. M. and Rasmussen, J. (1981). *Notes on human performance analysis* (Tech. Rep. Riso-M-2285). Denmark: Riso National Laboratory.

Hollnagel, E. (1998). Measurements and models, models and measurements: You can't have one without the other. In, *Proceedings of NATO AGARD conference,* Edinburgh, UK.

Hutchins, E. (1995). *Cognition in the wild.* Cambridge, MA: MIT Press.

Klein, G. (1998). *Sources of power: How people make decisions.* Cambridge, MA: MIT Press.

Langewiesche, W. (1998). *Inside the sky.* New York, NY: Random House.

Lanir, Z. (1986). *Fundamental surprise.* Eugene, OR: Decision Research.

McIntyre, J. A. (1994). Perspectives on human factors: The ISASI perspective. *Forum, 27,* 18.

Moshansky, V. P. (1992). *Commission of inquiry into the Air Ontario accident at Dryden, Ontario* (Final report, Vols. 1-4). Ottawa, ON: Minister of Supply and Services, Canada.

National Transportation Safety Board (1994). *Safety study, A review of flightcrew-involved major accidents of U.S. air carriers, 1978 through 1990* (NTSB/SS-94/01). Washington, DC: NTSB.

National Transportation Safety Board (1995). *Aircraft accident report: Flight into terrain during missed approach, USAir flight 1016, DC-9-31, N954VJ, Charlotte Douglas International Airport, Charlotte, North Carolina, July 2, 1994* (NTSB/AAR-95/03). Washington, DC: NTSB.

Neisser, U. (1976). *Cognition and reality.* San Francisco, CA: Freeman.

Orasanu, J., and Connolly, T. (1993). The reinvention of decision making. In, G.A. Klein, J. Orasanu, R. Calderwood and C. E. Zsambok (Eds.), *Decision making in action: Models and methods* (pp. 3-20). Norwood, NJ: Ablex.

Perrow, C. (1984). *Normal accidents.* New York, NY: Basic Books.

Rasmussen, J. and Batstone, R. (1989). *Why do complex organizational systems fail?* Environment Working Paper No. 20. Washington, DC: World Bank.
Reason, J. (1990). *Human error.* Cambridge, UK: Cambridge University Press.
Reason, J. (1997). *Managing the risks of organizational accidents.* Aldershot, UK: Ashgate.
Starbuck, W. H. and Milliken, F. J. (1988). Challenger: Fine-tuning the odds until something breaks. *Journal of management studies, 25,* 319-340.
Suchman, L. A. (1987). *Plans and situated actions: The problem of human-machine communication.* Cambridge, UK: Cambridge University Press.
Tuchman, B. W. (1981). *Practicing history: Selected essays.* New York, NY: Norton.
Varela, F. J., Thompson, E. and Rosch, E. (1995). *The embodied mind: Cognitive science and human experience.* Cambridge, MA: MIT Press.
Vaughan, D. (1996). *The Challenger launch decision.* Chicago, IL: University of Chicago Press.
Wagenaar, W. A. and Groeneweg, J. (1987). Accidents at sea: Multiple causes and impossible consequences. *International Journal of Man-Machine Studies, 27,* 587-589.
Weick, K. (1995). *Sensemaking in organizations.* London: Sage.
Willems, E. P. and Raush, H. L. (Eds.) (1969). *Naturalistic viewpoints in psychological research.* New York, NY: Holt, Rinehart and Winston.
Winograd, T. and Flores, F. (1987). *Understanding computers and cognition.* Reading, MA: Addison-Wesley.
Winograd, T. (1987). *Three responses to situation theory* (Technical report CSLI-87-106). Stanford, CA: Center for the study of language and information, Stanford University.
Woods, D. D. (1993). Process-tracing methods for the study of cognition outside of the experimental laboratory. In, G.A. Klein, J. Orasanu, R. Calderwood and C. E. Zsambok (Eds.), *Decision making in action: Models and methods* (pp. 228-251). Norwood, NJ: Ablex.
Woods, D. D., Johannesen, L. J., Cook, R. I. and Sarter, N. B. (1994). *Behind human error: Cognitive systems, computers and hindsight.* Dayton, OH: CSERIAC.

Acknowledgement

Work for this article was supported by a grant from the Swedish Flight Safety Directorate.

Applying Reason: the human factors analysis and classification system (HFACS)

Scott A. Shappell* and Douglas A. Wiegmann**
*Civil Aeromedical Institute, USA
**University of Illinois at Urbana-Champaign, USA

Abstract

Human error has been implicated in 70 to 80% of civil and military aviation accidents. Yet, most accident reporting systems are not designed around any theoretical framework of human error. As a result, most accident databases are not conducive to a traditional human error analysis, making the identification of intervention strategies onerous. What is required is a general human error framework around which new investigative methods can be designed and existing accident databases restructured. Toward these ends, a comprehensive human factors analysis and classification system (HFACS) has recently been developed to meet those needs. The HFACS framework has been used successfully within the military, commercial, and general aviation sectors to systematically examine underlying human causal factors and improve aviation accident investigations. This paper describes the development and theoretical underpinnings of HFACS in the hope that it will help safety professionals reduce the aviation accident rate through systematic, data-driven investment strategies and the objective evaluation of intervention programmes.

Introduction

Sadly, the annals of aviation history are littered with accidents and loss of life. Since the late 1950s, however, the drive to reduce the accident rate has yielded unprecedented levels of safety so that today it is safer to fly in a commercial airliner than to drive a car or even walk across a busy New York City street. Still,

Correspondence: Douglas A. Wiegmann, Aviation Research Lab, University of Illinois, #1 Airport Road, Savoy, IL 61874 or dwiegman@uiuc.edu while the aviation accident rate has declined impressively since the first flights nearly a century ago, the cost of aviation accidents in both lives and dollars has steadily risen. As a result, the effort to reduce the aviation accident rate still further has taken on a new meaning.

However, even with all the innovations and improvements realised in the last several decades, one fundamental question remains unanswered: 'Why do aircraft crash?' The answer may not be as straightforward as one might think. For example, in the early years of aviation, it could reasonably be said that, more often than not, the aircraft killed the pilot. That is, the aircraft were intrinsically unforgiving and, relative to their modern counterparts, mechanically unsafe. However, the modern era of aviation has witnessed an ironic reversal of sorts. It now appears to some that the aircrew themselves are more deadly than the aircraft they fly (Mason, 1993; cited in Murray, 1997). In fact, estimates in the literature indicate that between 70 and 80 % of aviation accidents can be attributed, at least in part, to human error (Shappell and Wiegmann, 1996).

So what really constitutes that 70-80 % of human error associated with aviation accidents? Some would have us believe that human error and 'pilot' error are synonymous. Yet, simply writing off aviation accidents merely to pilot error is an overly simplistic, if not naive, approach to accident causation. After all, it is well established that accidents cannot be attributed to a single cause, or in most instances, even a single individual (Heinrich, Petersen and Roos, 1980). In fact, even the identification of a 'primary' cause is fraught with problems. Instead, aviation accidents are the result of a number of causes, only the last of which are the unsafe acts of the aircrew (Reason, 1990; Shappell and Wiegmann, 1997a; Heinrich, Peterson and Roos, 1980; Bird, 1974).

The challenge for accident investigators and researchers alike is how best to identify and mitigate the causal sequence of events leading up to an accident, particularly that 70-80 % attributed to human error. Armed with this challenge, those interested in accident causation are left with a growing list of investigative schemes to chose from. In fact, there are nearly as many approaches to accident and error analysis as there are those involved in the process (Senders and Moray, 1991). Nevertheless, a comprehensive framework for identifying and analysing human error continues to elude safety professionals and theorists alike. Consequently, interventions cannot be accurately targeted at specific human causal factors nor can their effectiveness be objectively measured and assessed. Instead, safety professionals are left with interest/fad-driven research resulting in intervention strategies that peck around the edges of accident causation, but do little to reduce the overall accident rate (Wiegmann and Shappell, 1999). What is needed is a framework around which a needs-based, data-driven safety programme can be developed (Wiegmann and Shappell, 1997).

Purpose of the present paper

Recently, a comprehensive Human Factors Analysis and Classification System (HFACS) has been developed to meet those needs (Shappell and Wiegmann, 1998; Wiegmann and Shappell, 1998). This system, which is based on Reason's (1990) model of latent and active failures, is the result of several years of research and testing within both military and civilian aviation settings. The HFACS framework was originally developed for, and has recently been adopted by the U.S. Navy and Marine Corps as an accident investigation and data analysis tool. HFACS is also currently being employed by the U.S. Army and Air Force, and Canadian Forces, as well as the Federal Aviation Administration (FAA) and the National Aeronautics and Space Administration (NASA) as a complement to pre-existing systems. The purpose of the present paper, therefore is to describe the HFACS framework and its underlying theoretical foundation, as well as to summarise the empirical research supporting its utility as an error analysis and accident investigation framework.

The human factors analysis and classification system

In perhaps one of the most widely cited books in the field, Jim Reason (1990) described four levels of human failure within an organisation, each influencing the next in the genesis of accidents (Figure 1). In many ways, Reason's 'Swiss cheese' model of accident causation revolutionised common views on the subject. Unfortunately, however, Reason's model is mainly a theory with few details on how to apply it in real-world settings. In other words, the theory never described what the 'holes in the cheese' really are so they can be identified during accident investigations or better yet, detected and corrected before an accident occurs. To remedy this, the HFACS framework was developed to apply Reason's conceptual model by describing the holes at each of four levels of human failure: 1) Unsafe Acts, 2) Preconditions for Unsafe Acts, 3) Unsafe Supervision, and 4) Organisational Influences. A description of the major components and causal categories follows, beginning with the level most closely tied to the accident – the unsafe acts of operators.

Unsafe acts

Working backward in time from the accident, the first level of HFACS describes those *unsafe acts* of operators that led to the accident. More commonly referred to in aviation as aircrew/pilot error, this level is where most accident investigations are focused and consequently, where the majority of causal factors are uncovered. The unsafe acts of aircrew can be loosely classified into two categories: errors and violations (Reason, 1990). In general, errors represent the mental or physical activities of individuals that fail to achieve their intended outcome. Violations, on the other hand, refer to the wilful disregard for the rules and regulations. However, merely distinguishing between errors and violations does not provide the level of granularity required of most error analyses and accident investigations. Therefore, the categories of errors and violations were expanded here (Figure 2), as elsewhere (Reason, 1990; Rasmussen, 1982), to include three basic error types (skill-based, decision, and perceptual) and two forms of violations (routine and exceptional).

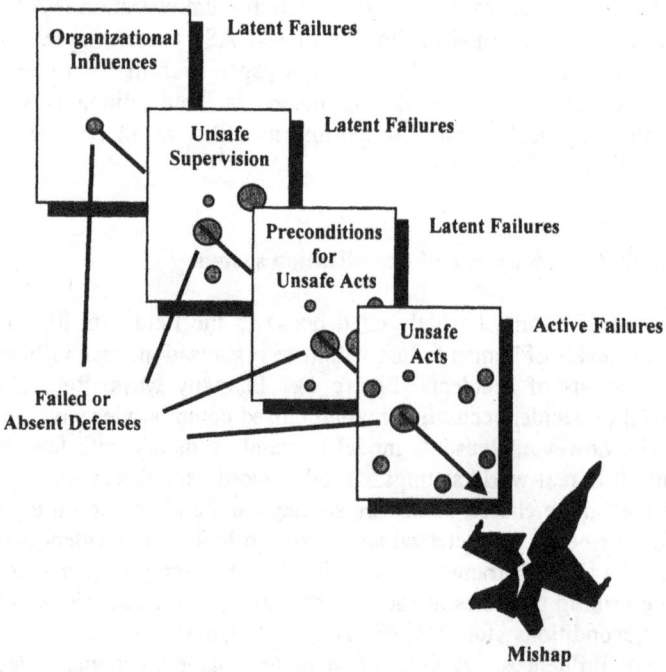

Figure 1 The 'Swiss cheese' model of human error causation (adapted from Reason, 1990)

Errors

Skill-based errors Within the context of aviation, skill-based behaviour is best described as 'stick-and-rudder' and other basic flight activities that occur without significant conscious thought. As a result, these skill-based actions are particularly vulnerable to failures of attention and/or memory. In fact, attention failures have been linked to many skill-based errors such as the breakdown in visual scan patterns, task fixation, and the inadvertent activation of controls (Table 1). Consider, for example, a crew that becomes so fixated on trouble-shooting a burned out warning light that they fail to monitor their altimeter and fatally descends into the terrain. Perhaps a bit closer to home, consider the unfortunate soul who locks him/herself out of the car or misses their exit because they were either distracted, in a hurry, or daydreaming. These are both examples of attention failures that commonly occur during highly automated behaviour. While at home or driving around town, these attention failures may merely be frustrating. However, in the air they can become catastrophic.

Table 1 Selected examples of Unsafe Acts of Pilot Operators (Note: This is not a complete listing)

Errors	Violations
Skill-based Errors	Failed to adhere to brief
Breakdown in visual scan	Failed to use the radar altimeter
Failed to prioritise attention	Flew an unauthorised approach
Inadvertent use of flight controls	Violated training rules
Omitted step in procedure	Flew an overaggressive manoeuvre
Omitted checklist item	Failed to properly prepare for the flight
Poor technique	
Over-controlled the aircraft	Briefed unauthorised flight
	Not current/qualified for the mission
Decision Errors	Intentionally exceeded the limits of the aircraft
Improper procedure	
Misdiagnosed emergency	Continued low-altitude flight in VMC
Wrong response to emergency	
Exceeded ability	Unauthorised low-altitude canyon running
Inappropriate manoeuvre	
Poor decision	
Perceptual Errors (due to)	
Misjudged distance/altitude/airspeed	
Spatial disorientation	
Visual illusion	

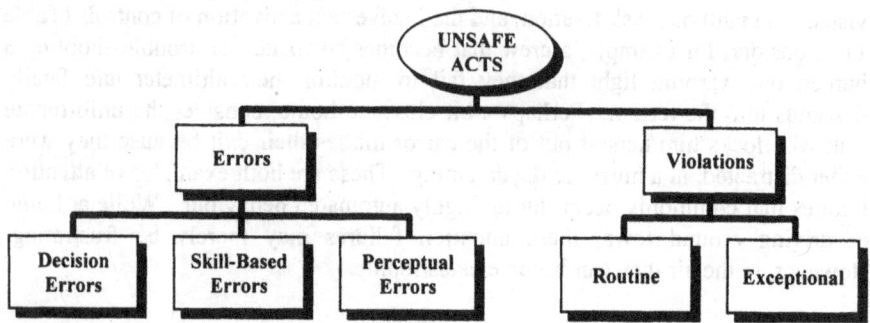

Figure 2 Categories of unsafe acts committed by aircrews

In contrast, memory failures often appear as omitted items in a checklist, place losing, or forgotten intentions. For example, many of us have forgotten to replace the gas cap after refuelling the family car or failed to put the coffee in the coffee-pot before turning it on. Likewise, it is not difficult to imagine that when under the stress of an in-flight emergency for example or after a long, fatiguing flight, critical steps/procedures can be missed. Yet, even when not particularly stressed, individuals have forgotten to set the flaps on approach or lower the landing gear – at a minimum, an embarrassing gaffe.

The third class of skill-based errors involves the manner, or technique, individuals employ while controlling their aircraft. For example, two pilots with identical training, flight grades, and experience may differ significantly in the way they fly. That is, some pilots may fly smooth and effortlessly, while others are more forceful and rough on the flight controls. Both may be safe and equally proficient in the air; however, given certain scenarios the techniques they employ could set them up for failure. Ultimately, such techniques are as much a factor of innate ability and aptitude as they are an overt expression of one's personality, making efforts at the prevention and mitigation of technique errors particularly difficult.

Decision errors Perhaps the most heavily investigated of all error forms, decision errors represent intentional behaviour that proceeds as intended, yet the plan proves inadequate or inappropriate for the situation. Often referred to as 'honest mistakes,' this type of error can generally be grouped into one of three categories: procedural errors, choice errors, and problem solving errors (Table 1). Procedural decision errors (Orasanu, 1993), or rule-based mistakes as described by Rasmussen (1982), occur during highly structured tasks of the sorts, if X, then do Y. Aviation, particularly within the military and commercial sectors, by its very nature is highly structured, and consequently, much of pilot decision making is procedural. In fact, there are very explicit procedures to be performed at virtually all phases of flight. Still, errors can, and often do, occur when a situation is either not recognised or misdiagnosed, and the wrong procedure is applied.

Even in aviation however, not all situations have corresponding procedures that address them. Instead, many situations require that a choice be made among multiple response options. Consider for instance the pilot who unexpectedly confronts a line of thunderstorms directly along the flight path. He or she can choose to fly around the weather, divert to another field until the weather passes, or penetrate the weather hoping to quickly transition through it. When confronted with situations such as these, choice decision errors (Orasanu, 1993), or knowledge-based mistakes as they are otherwise known (Rasmussen, 1986), may occur. This is particularly true when there is insufficient experience, time, or other outside pressures that may preclude correct decisions. Put simply, sometimes individuals chose well, and sometimes they don't.

Finally, there are occasions when a problem is not well understood, and formal procedures or response options are not available. It is during these ill-defined situations that the construction of a novel solution is required. In a sense, individuals find themselves where no one has been before, and in many ways, must 'fly by the seats of their pants.' Individuals placed in this situation must resort to slow and effortful reasoning processes where time is a luxury rarely afforded. Consequently, while this type of decision making is more infrequent then other forms, the relative proportion of errors committed is markedly higher.

Perceptual error Not unexpectedly, when one's perception of the world differs from reality, errors can, and often do, occur. Typically, perceptual errors occur when sensory input is either degraded or 'unusual', as is the case with visual illusions and spatial disorientation (Table 1). Visual illusions, for example, occur when the brain tries to 'fill in the gaps' with what it feels belongs in a visually impoverished environment, like that seen at night or when flying in adverse weather. Likewise, spatial disorientation occurs when the vestibular system cannot resolve one's orientation in space and therefore must make a 'best guess' typically when normal visual (horizon) cues are absent. In either event, the unsuspecting individual often is left to make a decision based on a faulty perception of the situation where the potential for committing an error is exacerbated.

It is important to note, however, that it is not the illusion or disorientation that is classified as a perceptual error. Rather, it is the pilot's erroneous response to the illusion or disorientation. For example, many pilots have experienced spatial disorientation (often referred to as the 'leans') when flying into the weather. However, in instances such as these, pilots are taught to rely on their primary instruments, rather than their senses when controlling the aircraft. Nevertheless, some pilots fail to monitor their instruments when flying in adverse weather or at night when visual cues are minimal. Unfortunately, these aircrew and others who have been fooled by illusions and other disorientating flight regimes may end up involved in an aircraft accident, many of which prove fatal.

Violations

By definition, errors occur while aircrew are behaving within the rules and regulations implemented by an organisation and typically dominate most accident databases. In contrast, violations represent the wilful disregard for the rules and regulations that govern safe flight and, fortunately, occur much less frequently (Shappell et al., 1999b).

While there are many ways to distinguish between types of violations, two distinct forms have been identified, based on their aetiology (Table 1). The first, routine violations, tend to be habitual by nature and are often tolerated by governing authority (Reason, 1990). Consider, for example, the individual who drives consistently 5-10 mph faster than allowed by law or someone who routinely flies in marginal weather when authorised for visual meteorological conditions only. While both certainly violate governing regulations, many drivers or pilots do the same thing. Furthermore, people who drive 64 mph in a 55-mph zone, almost always drive 64 in a 55-mph zone. That is, they 'routinely' violate the speed limit. The same can typically be said of the pilot who routinely flies into marginal weather.

Often referred to as 'bending the rules', these violations are often tolerated and, in effect, sanctioned by authority (i.e., you're not likely to get a traffic citation until you exceed the posted speed limit by more than 10 mph). If, however, local authorities started handing out traffic citations for exceeding the speed limit on the highway by 9 mph or less, then it is less likely that individuals would violate the rules. By definition then, if a routine violation is identified, investigators must look further up the causal chain to identify those individuals in authority who are not enforcing the rules.

In contrast, exceptional violations appear as isolated departures from authority, not necessarily characteristic of an individual's typical behaviour pattern nor condoned by management (Reason, 1990). For example, an isolated instance of driving 105 mph in a 55 mph zone is considered an exceptional violation. Likewise, flying under a bridge or engaging in other particularly dangerous and prohibited manoeuvres would constitute an exceptional violation. However, it is important to note that, while most exceptional violations are appalling, they are not considered 'exceptional' because of their extreme nature. Rather, they are considered exceptional because they are neither typical of the individual nor condoned by authority. Unfortunately, the unexpected nature of exceptional violations make them particularly difficult to predict and problematic for organisations to deal with.

Preconditions for unsafe acts

What makes Reason's (1990) 'Swiss cheese' model particularly useful in accident investigation, is that it encourages investigators to address the latent failures within the causal sequence of events as well as the more obvious active failures described above. As their name suggests, latent failures, unlike their active counterparts, may lie dormant or undetected for hours, days, weeks, or even longer, until one day they adversely affect the unsuspecting aircrew. Historically, such latent failures have often been overlooked by investigators largely because the types of latent failures or 'holes in the cheese' that adversely affect aircrew performance have not been clearly defined. To remedy this, the HFACS framework describes the first layer of latent conditions, *Preconditions for Unsafe Acts*, within the context of substandard conditions of operators and the substandard practices they perform (Figure 3).

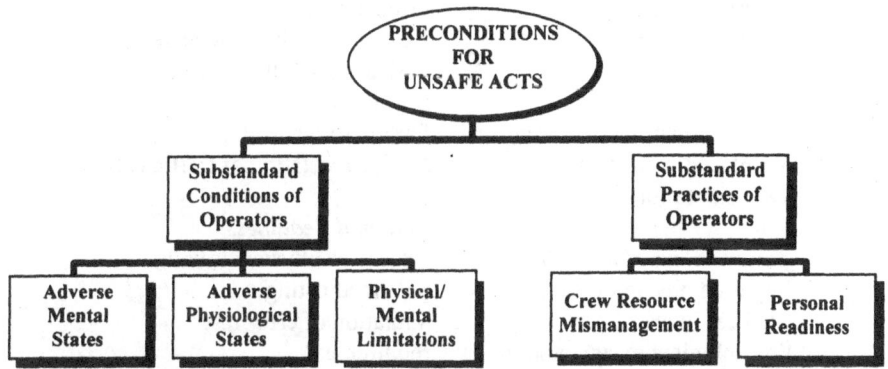

Figure 3 Categories of preconditions of unsafe acts

Substandard conditions of operators

Adverse mental states   Being prepared mentally is critical in nearly every endeavour, but perhaps even more so in aviation. As such, the category of Adverse Mental States was created to account for those mental conditions that affect performance (Table 2). Principal among these are the loss of situational awareness, task fixation, distraction, and *mental* fatigue due to sleep loss or other stressors. Also included here are personality traits and pernicious attitudes such as overconfidence, complacency, and misplaced motivation.

Consider, for example, the individual who is mentally fatigued or suffering the effects of sleep loss. The likelihood that an error will occur given these preconditions becomes much more predictable. In a similar manner, overconfidence and other pernicious attitudes such as arrogance and impulsivity will influence the likelihood that a violation will be committed. Clearly then, any framework of human error must account for these pre-existing adverse mental states if a thorough understanding of the causal chain of events is to be realised.

Table 2 Selected examples of Unsafe Aircrew Conditions (Note: This is not a complete listing)

Substandard Conditions of Operators	Substandard Practice of Operators
Adverse Mental States	*Crew Resource Management*
Channelized attention	Failed to back-up
Complacency	Failed to communicate/co-ordinate
Distraction	
Mental fatigue	Failed to conduct adequate brief
Get-home-it is	Failed to use all available resources
Haste	
Loss of situational awareness	Failure of leadership
Misplaced motivation	Misinterpretation of traffic calls
Task saturation	
	Personal Readiness
Adverse Physiological States	Excessive physical training
Impaired physiological state	Self-medicating
Medical illness	Violation of crew rest requirement
Physiological incapacitation	
Physical fatigue	Violation of bottle-to-throttle requirement
Spatial Disorientation	
Visual Illusions	
Physical/Mental Limitation	
Insufficient reaction time	
Visual limitation	
Incompatible intelligence/aptitude	
Incompatible physical capability	

Adverse physiological states The second category, adverse physiological states, refers to those medical or physiological conditions that interfere with safe operations (Table 2). Particularly important to aviation are such conditions as visual illusions and spatial disorientation as described earlier, as well as *physical* fatigue, and the myriad of pharmacological and medical abnormalities known to affect performance.

The effects of visual illusions and spatial disorientation are well known to most aviators. However, less well known to aviators, and often overlooked are the effects of simply being ill on cockpit performance. Nearly all of us have gone to work ill, dosed with over-the-counter medications, and have generally performed well. Consider however, the pilot suffering from the common head cold. Unfortunately, most aviators view a head cold as only a minor inconvenience that can be easily remedied using over-the counter antihistamines, acetaminophen, and other non-prescription medications. In fact, when confronted with a stuffy nose, aviators typically are only concerned with the effects of a painful sinus block as cabin altitude changes. However, it is not the overt symptoms that flight surgeons are concerned with. Rather, it is the accompanying inner ear infection and the increased likelihood of spatial disorientation when entering instrument meteorological conditions that is alarming - not to mention the side-effects of antihistamines, fatigue, and sleep loss on pilot decision-making. Therefore, it is incumbent upon any safety professional to account for these sometimes subtle adverse physiological states as well as other more obvious ones such as spatial disorientation and visual illusions within the causal chain of events.

Physical/mental limitations The final class of substandard conditions involves individual physical/mental limitations (Table 2). Specifically, this category refers to those instances when mission requirements exceed the capabilities of the individual at the controls. For example, the human visual system is severely limited at night; yet, when driving an automobile, many drivers do not necessarily slow down or take additional precautions. Likewise, in aviation, while slowing down is not necessarily an option, increasing one's vigilance for other aircraft or obstacles whose size or contrast interferes with their detection will often increase the safety margin.

Similarly, there are occasions when the time required to complete a task or manoeuvre exceeds an individual's capacity. That is, while good pilots are typically noted for their ability to respond quickly and accurately, individuals vary widely in their ability to process and respond to information. Still, even given individual differences, if any operator or pilot is required to respond quickly (as is the case in many aviation emergencies), the probability of making an error will likely increase.

In addition to the basic sensory and information processing limitations described above, there are at least two additional instances of physical/mental limitations that need to be addressed, albeit they are often overlooked by most safety professionals. These limitations involve individuals who simply are not compatible with aviation, because they are either unsuited physically or do not possess the aptitude to fly. For example, some individuals simply don't have the physical strength or dexterity to operate in the unique aviation environment, or for anthropometric reasons, simply have difficulty reaching the controls. In other words, cockpits have traditionally not been designed with all shapes, sizes, and physical abilities in mind.

Likewise, not everyone has the mental ability or aptitude for flying aircraft. Just as not all of us can be concert pianists or NFL linebackers, not everyone has the innate ability to pilot an aircraft – a vocation that requires the unique ability to make decisions quickly and respond accurately in life threatening situations. The difficult task for the safety professional is determining whether physical abilities or aptitude might have contributed to the accident causal sequence.

Substandard practices of operators

Clearly then, numerous substandard conditions of operators can, and do, lead to the commission of unsafe acts. Nevertheless, there are a number of things that individuals do to themselves that set up these substandard conditions. Generally speaking, the substandard practices of operators can be summed up in two categories: crew resource mismanagement and personal readiness.

Crew resource mismanagement Good communication skills and team co-ordination has been the mantra of industrial/organisational and personnel psychology for decades. Not surprising then, crew resource management has been a cornerstone of aviation for the last few decades (Helmreich and Foushee, 1993; Wiegmann and Shappell, 1999). As a result, the category of crew resource mismanagement was created to account for occurrences of poor co-ordination among personnel (Table 2). Within the context of aviation, this includes co-ordination both within and between aircraft, with air traffic control facilities and maintenance control, as well as with facility and other support personnel as necessary. Likewise, good crew resource management includes co-ordination before and after the flight in the form of pre-flight briefings and debriefings as necessary.

Unfortunately, the history of aviation is replete with instances where the lack of crew co-ordination has led to confusion and poor decision making in the cockpit, resulting in an accident (Wiegmann and Shappell, 1999). One of the more notable failures of crew resource management within the commercial airline industry was the crash of a civilian airliner at night in the Florida Everglades in 1972 (NTSB, 1973). It seems the crew was busily trying to troubleshoot what amounted to a burnt out indicator light, and no one was monitoring the aircraft's altitude as the altitude hold was inadvertently disconnected. Ideally, the crew would have co-ordinated the trouble-shooting task ensuring that at least one crewmember was monitoring basic flight instruments and 'flying' the aircraft. Regrettably, this wasn't the case, as they entered a slow, unrecognised descent, into the Florida Everglades resulting in numerous fatalities.

Personal readiness In aviation, or for that matter in any occupational setting, individuals are expected to show up for work ready to perform at optimal levels. Nevertheless, in aviation as in other professions, personal readiness failures occur when individuals fail to prepare physically or mentally for duty (Table 2). For instance, violations of crew rest requirements, bottle-to-brief rules, and self-medicating all will affect performance on the job and are particularly detrimental in the aircraft. Not surprising for example, when individuals violate crew rest requirements, they run the risk of mental fatigue and other adverse mental states, which may ultimately lead to errors and accidents. Note however, that violations that affect personal readiness are not considered 'unsafe act, violations' since they typically do not happen in the cockpit, nor are they necessarily active failures with direct and immediate consequences.

Still, not all personal readiness failures occur as a result of violations of governing rules or regulations. For example, running 10 miles before piloting an aircraft may not be against any existing regulations, yet it may impair the physical and mental capabilities of the individual enough to degrade performance and elicit unsafe acts. Likewise, the traditional 'candy bar and coke' lunch of the modern military pilot may sound good but may not be sufficient to sustain performance in the rigorous environment of aviation. While there may be no rules governing such behaviour, pilots must use good judgement when deciding whether they are 'fit' to fly an aircraft.

Unsafe supervision

Exactly why do preconditions for unsafe acts exist in the first place? This is perhaps where Reason's work departed from the more traditional engineering approaches when addressing human error. Specifically, Reason traced the circumstances, or causal chain of events, producing unsafe acts up the supervisory chain of command, beginning with front-line supervisors. Referred to as *Unsafe Supervision*, the third level of human failure can be parsed into four broad categories: inadequate supervision, planned inappropriate operations, failure to correct a known problem, and supervisory violations (Figure 4).

Inadequate supervision Put simply, the role of any supervisor is to provide the opportunity to succeed. To do this, supervisors must provide guidance, training opportunities, leadership, motivation and oversight to their subordinates (Table 3). Unfortunately, this is not always the case. For example, it is not difficult to conceive of a situation where adequate crew resource management training was either not provided, or the opportunity to attend such training was not afforded to a particular aircrew member. Consequently, aircrew co-ordination skills could be compromised and if the aircraft were put into an adverse situation (an emergency for instance), the risk of an error being committed would be magnified.

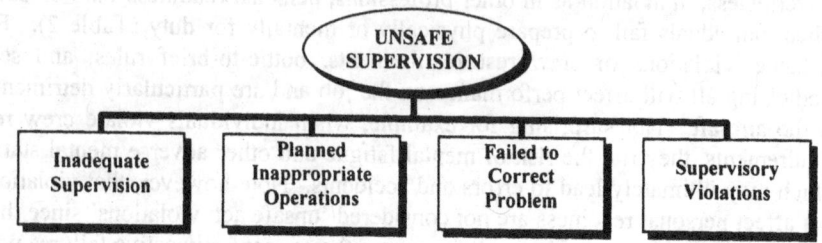

Figure 4   Categories of unsafe supervision

Likewise, sound professional guidance and oversight are essential ingredients of any successful organisation. While empowering individuals to make decisions and function independently are certainly essential, this does not divorce the supervisor from accountability. For instance, the lack of guidance and oversight has proven to be the breeding ground for many of the violations that have crept into the cockpit. Consequently, any thorough investigation of accident causal factors must consider the role supervision plays (i.e., whether the supervision was inappropriate or did not occur at all) in the genesis of human error.

Planned inappropriate operations Occasionally, the operational tempo and/or the scheduling of aircrew are such that individuals are put at unacceptable risk, crew rest is jeopardised, and ultimately performance is adversely affected. Such operations, though arguably unavoidable during emergencies, are unacceptable during normal operations. As a result, the second category of unsafe supervision, planned inappropriate operations, was created to account for these failures (Table 3).

Consider, for example, the issue of improper crew pairing. It is well known that when very senior, dictatorial captains are paired with very junior, weak co-pilots, communication and co-ordination problems are likely to occur. Commonly referred to as the trans-cockpit authority gradient, such conditions likely contributed to the fatal crash of a commercial airliner into the Potomac River outside of Washington, DC, in January of 1982 (NTSB, 1982). In that accident, the captain of the aircraft repeatedly rebuffed the first officer when the latter indicated that the engine instruments did not appear normal. Nevertheless, the captain continued a fatal takeoff in icing conditions with less than adequate takeoff thrust. As a result, the aircraft stalled and crashed into the icy river, killing the crew and many of the passengers.

Table 3 Selected examples of Unsafe Supervision (Note: This is not a complete listing)

Inadequate Supervision	*Failed to Correct a Known Problem*
Failed to provide guidance	Failed to correct document in error
Failed to provide operational doctrine	Failed to identify an at-risk aviator
Failed to provide oversight	Failed to initiate corrective action
Failed to provide training	Failed to report unsafe tendencies
Failed to track qualifications	
Failed to track performance	*Supervisory Violations*
	Authorised unnecessary hazard
Planned Inappropriate Operations	Failed to enforce rules and regulations
Failed to provide correct data	Authorised unqualified crew for flight
Failed to provide adequate brief time	
Improper manning	
Mission not in accordance with rules/regulations	
Provided inadequate opportunity for crew rest	

Clearly, the captain and crew were held accountable - they died in the accident. Nevertheless, what was the role of the supervisory chain? Perhaps crew pairing was equally responsible. Although not specifically addressed in the report, such issues are clearly worth exploring in many accidents. In fact, in that particular accident, several other training and manning issues were identified that would arguably be considered unsafe supervision here.

Failure to correct a known problem The third category, failed to correct a known problem, refers to those instances when deficiencies among individuals, equipment, training or other related safety areas are 'known' to the supervisor, yet are allowed to continue unabated (Table 3). For example, it is not uncommon for accident investigators to interview the pilot's friends, colleagues, and supervisors after a fatal crash only to find out that they 'knew it would happen to him some day.' If the supervisor knew that a pilot was incapable of flying safely, and allowed the flight anyway, he clearly did the pilot no favours. The failure to correct the behaviour, either through remedial training or, if necessary, removal from flight status, in effect sealed the fate of the pilot - not to mention the others who may have been on board.

Likewise, the failure to consistently correct or discipline inappropriate behaviour fosters an unsafe atmosphere and promotes the violation of rules. Aviation history is rich with reports of aviators who tell hair-raising stories of their exploits and barnstorming low-level flights (the infamous 'been there, done that'). While entertaining to some, they often serve to promulgate a perception of tolerance and 'one-up-manship' until one day someone pays the price. Ultimately, failures such as these committed by supervisors have played a significant role in accident causation.

Supervisory violations Although arguably rare, supervisors have been known to violate the rules and doctrine when managing their assets prompting a category to account for these failures (Table 3). For example, allowing unqualified individuals to fly in adverse weather conditions or pressuring crews to overlook safety precautions in the interest of time and profit have both lead to accidents. Likewise, it can be argued that failing to enforce existing rules and regulations or flaunting authority are also violations at the supervisory level. While rare and possibly difficult to cull out, such practices invariably set the stage for the sequence of events that predictably follow.

Organisational influences

Reason's model didn't stop at the supervisory level either. In fact, fallible decisions of upper-level management directly affect supervisory practices, as well as the conditions and actions of operators. Therefore, it makes sense that, if the accident rate is going to be reduced beyond current levels, investigators and analysts alike must examine the accident sequence in its entirety, including the organisation as a whole. Unfortunately, these organisational failures often go unnoticed by safety professionals, due in large part to the lack of a clear framework from which to investigate them. With this in mind, the HFACS framework was designed to capture the most elusive of these latent failures including resource management, organisational climate, and operational processes (Figure 5).

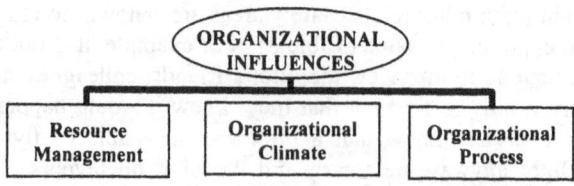

Figure 5 Organisational factors influencing accidents

Resource management This category encompasses the realm of corporate-level decision making regarding the allocation and maintenance of organisational assets such as human resources (personnel), monetary assets, and equipment/facilities (Table 4). Generally speaking, corporate decisions about how such resources should be managed centre around two distinct objectives – the goal of safety and the goal of on-time, cost-effective operations. In times of prosperity, both objectives can be easily balanced and satisfied in full. However, there may also be times of fiscal austerity that demand some give-and-take between the two. Unfortunately, history tells us that safety is often the loser in such battles and safety and training are often the first to be cut in organisations having financial difficulties.

Excessive cost cutting can also result in reduced funding for new equipment or may lead to the purchase of equipment that is sub-optimal and inadequately designed for the type of operations flown by the company. Other trickle-down effects include poorly maintained equipment and workspaces, and the failure to correct known design flaws in existing equipment. The result is a scenario involving unseasoned, less-skilled pilots flying old and poorly maintained aircraft under the least desirable conditions and schedules, all effecting the delicate balance between safety and profit.

Organisational climate This category refers to a broad class of organisational variables that influence worker performance (Table 4). Formally, it was defined as the 'situationally based consistencies in the organisation's treatment of individuals' (Jones, 1988). In general, however, organisational climate can be viewed as the working atmosphere within the organisation. One telltale sign of an organisation's climate is its structure, as reflected in the chain-of-command, delegation of authority and responsibility, communication channels, and formal accountability for actions. Just like in the cockpit, communication and co-ordination are vital within an organisation. If management and staff within an organisation are not communicating, or if no one knows who is in charge, organisational safety clearly suffers and accidents do happen (Muchinsky, 1997).

An organisation's policies and culture are also good indicators of its climate. Policies are official guidelines that direct management's decisions about such things as hiring and firing, promotion, retention, raises, sick leave, and other day-to-day operations. Culture, on the other hand, refers to the unofficial or unspoken rules, values, attitudes, beliefs, and customs of an organisation – sort of 'the way things really get done around here.' Regardless, when policies are ill-defined, adversarial, or conflicting, or when they are supplanted by unofficial rules and values, confusion abounds within the organisation. Ultimately, safety is bound to suffer under such conditions.

Operational process The final category, operational process, refers to corporate decisions and rules that govern everyday activities within an organisation. Specifically, such processes as the establishment and use of standardised operating procedures and formal methods for maintaining checks and balances (oversight) between the workforce and management is included here (Table 4). It is not difficult to envision instances when those within the upper echelon of an organisation determine that it is necessary to increase the operational tempo to a point that overextends a supervisor's staffing capabilities. Therefore, a supervisor may resort to the use of inadequate scheduling procedures that jeopardise crew rest and produce sub-optimal crew pairings, putting aircrew at increased risk.

Table 4   Selected examples of Organisational Influences (Note: This is not a complete listing)

Resource/Acquisition Management	Organisational Process
Human Resources	*Operations*
Selection	Operational tempo
Staffing/manning	Time pressure
Training	Production quotas
Monetary/budget resources	Incentives
Excessive cost cutting	Measurement/appraisal
Lack of funding	Schedules
Equipment/facility resources	Deficient planning
Poor design	
Purchasing of unsuitable equipment	*Procedures*
	Standards
	Clearly defined objectives
Organisational Climate	Documentation
	Instructions
Structure	
Chain-of-command	*Oversight*
Delegation of authority	Risk management
Communication	Safety programmes
Formal accountability for actions	
Policies	
Hiring and firing	
Promotion	
Drugs and alcohol	
Culture	
Norms and rules	
Values and beliefs	
Organisational justice	

Regrettably, not all organisations have procedures in place to address such contingencies nor do they engage in an active process of monitoring aircrew errors and human factor problems via anonymous reporting systems and safety audits. As such, supervisors and managers are often unaware of the problems before an accident occurs. Indeed, it has been said that 'an accident is one incident too many' (Reinhart, 1996). It is incumbent upon any organisation to fervently seek out the 'holes in the cheese' and plug them up, before they create a window of opportunity for catastrophe to strike.

Evaluating the framework

Clearly, HFACS or any other framework only contributes to an already burgeoning list of human error taxonomies if it does not prove useful in the operational setting. Therefore, to ensure that the HFACS taxonomy would have utility as an accident investigation and data analysis tool, and is not merely the result of a long academic exercise, it was designed around an explicit set of criteria. Specifically, five criteria were used throughout the development process: comprehensiveness, diagnosticity, reliability, usability, and validity (Hollnagel, 1998; O'Connor and Hardiman 1996).

Comprehensiveness

In this context, comprehensiveness refers to the extent to which an error taxonomy captures all the information surrounding an error or accident (O'Connor and Hardiman, 1996). Assessing comprehensiveness is a reiterative process that involves mapping frameworks onto existing accident databases to identify if any human causal factors are left unaccounted for. Our early efforts to develop a comprehensive human error taxonomy (Shappell and Wiegmann, 1995; Wiegmann and Shappell, 1995; Wiegmann and Shappell, 1997) involved testing error frameworks already existing in the literature against the U.S. Navy/Marine Corps aviation accident database. These exiting frameworks, however, focused primarily on the information processing or unsafe acts level of operator performance, and missed several other key human factors considered causal to many of the accidents. Consequently, a new error taxonomy, was developed to capture the preconditions and unsafe supervisory factors associated with many of these accidents (Shappell and Wiegmann, 1997a).

The Taxonomy of Unsafe Operations, as it was originally called, was then tested against the U.S. Navy/Marine Corps aviation accident database and others made available by military (U.S. Army Safety Center and U.S. Air Force Safety Center) and civilian organisations (National Transportation Safety Board). Again, however, additional latent organisational factors were found that remained unaccounted for by the framework and further modifications were required. The resulting taxonomy was the HFACS framework described here (Shappell and Wiegmann, 1998; Wiegmann and Shappell, 1998).

The HFACS framework was once again mapped onto each of these military and civilian databases, resulting in a complete capture of the human-causal factors contributing to operator error in these data sources (Shappell and Wiegmann, 1999). Since then, evaluations of the comprehensiveness of HFACS have also been performed using error data from other contexts (e.g., aircraft maintenance and air traffic control). The results of these efforts suggest that the taxonomy is robust and complete in its error categories with regard to the types of errors that occur in other operational settings as well (Schmidt, 1998; Pounds, et al., 1999).

Diagnosticity

For years the U.S. Navy/Marine Corps, like other military and civilian organisations, has been limited to reporting aviation accident trends as rates (accidents per 100,000 flight hours) which included all types of accidents regardless of causal genesis. That is, accidents due to human error have not been differentiated from those due to other non-human causal factors such as mechanical failures and environmental conditions. As such, the extent to which human error has been analysed has been to simply report that human error is associated with 60-80% of aviation accidents making intervention strategies difficult to identify, implement, and evaluate (Wiegmann and Shappell, 1997).

To be useful then, an error taxonomy must have good diagnosticity. That is, it must be able to identify relationships between errors and to penetrate all levels of the system in such a way that previously unforeseen accident trends or causes are revealed (O'Connor and Hardiman, 1996). Diagnosticity also refers to the sensitivity of a taxonomy to changes in error trends, allowing for the successful assessment and monitoring of selected interventions strategies.

Recently for example, 181 U.S. Navy and Marine Corps tactical aircraft (TACAIR) and helicopter accidents occurring between fiscal years 1991 to 1997 were analysed using HFACS (Shappell et al., 1999). Of these 181 accidents, 35% were associated with at least one violation of the rules and regulations. To put these numbers into perspective, a similar HFACS analysis was also performed on U.S. Army and U.S. Air Force aviation accident data. A comparison across similar types of aircraft revealed that during roughly this same time frame, violations were identified in 27% (17 of 62 accidents) of the U.S. Army accidents examined and only 7% (5 of 67 accidents) of those in the U.S. Air Force. Because of this analysis, the U.S. Navy/Marine Corps underwent a programme designed to specifically reduce this particular unsafe act among Naval aviators.

One potentially viable intervention might have been to punish the violators or even to remove them from flight status so that they (or others) would not repeat the offence. However, a closer examination of the data revealed that the majority of violations associated with these accidents were considered 'routine' by HFACS standards (i.e., habitual actions often associated with unsafe supervisory conditions). Consequently, intervention strategies that incorporated the supervisory chain as well as the aircrew were needed. Therefore, in late 1997 the US Navy/Marine Corps embarked on an organised agenda to promote supervision, professionalism, accountability, and enforcement of the rules to mitigate violations in the fleet. Subsequent HFACS analyses revealed that by fiscal year 1998 the Navy/Marine Corps had nearly halved its percentage of accidents associated with violations to approximately 17% and that this trend has continued into fiscal year 1999 (Neubauer, Murdock, Fraser and Veronneau, 1999).

A second illustration of the HFACS framework's diagnosticity involves the issue of aviator readiness/proficiency. Given the drawdown within the military over the last several years and the marked reduction in flight hours, there has been a growing concern regarding a concomitant reduction in the proficiency of our aircrews. Translated into HFACS terminology, these monetary and training cutbacks are an organisational, resource management issue, whereas proficiency is best defined within the context of skill-based errors. Recall that skill-based behaviour in the cockpit typically refers to those stick-and-rudder and other basic flight skills (e.g., instrument and out of cockpit scan patterns) that are highly practised and typically occur without much conscious thought.

To the extent that skill-based errors are a measure of proficiency, it would seem logical to examine the percentage of accidents associated with skill-based errors across the years of this military drawdown. Indeed, an HFACS analysis of TACAIR and Rotary Wing accidents since 1991 (Shappell, et al., 1999) revealed a steady rise in the percentage of accidents associated with skill-based errors over the last eight years, suggesting a steady erosion in proficiency. Unfortunately, intervention strategies for improving proficiency are not nearly as clear cut as those associated with violations. Nevertheless, the HFACS framework suggests that any intervention will need to re-emphasise the basics tenets of flying, including efficient instrument scan, prioritising attention, recognising extremis situations, basic flight skills (Stick-and-Rudder). The extent to which these interventions are effectively implemented and funded by upper level management and thus directly impact proficiency will have to be assessed through future HFACS analysis of error and accident data.

With regard to diagnosticity then, the HFACS framework has been found to be an effective instrument, having utility as both an error analysis and intervention assessment tool. Other illustrations not discussed here (e.g., Shappell and Wiegmann, 1997b; Wiegmann and Shappell, 1999) include evaluations of such intervention programmes as ground proximity warning systems (GPWS) to prevent controlled flight into terrain (CFIT), as well as aircrew co-ordination training to prevent CRM errors in the cockpit. In general, these and other systematic applications of HFACS to the analysis of human factors accident data have afforded the U.S. Navy/Marine Corps (for which the original taxonomy was developed) the ability to develop objective, data-driven intervention strategies. In a sense, HFACS has illuminated those areas ripe for intervention rather than relying on individual research interests not necessarily tied to saving lives or preventing aircraft losses.

Reliability

According to O'Connor and Hardiman (1996), an error framework should produce reliable insights, such that its application results in different users discovering similar factors associated with the same accident or error event. Similar to assessing comprehensiveness, evaluating and improving the reliability of a taxonomic system is also a reiterative process. Specifically, the process involves assessing initial levels of inter-rater agreements, then modifying error categories, definitions, or instructions if necessary and reassessing agreement levels (usually using a new data set) to determine if reliabilities have improved to an acceptable level. Although there are several formulas for assessing reliability, Cohen's Kappa is generally regarded as the best index of inter-rater agreement for error classification or other similar tasks (see Primavara, Allison, and Alfonso, 1996 for review of methods for quantifying reliability). Cohen's Kappa is an index of agreement that has been corrected for chance. By conventional standards, index values of .60 to .74 are considered 'good' and values of .75 or higher are considered 'excellent' levels of agreement (Fleiss, 1981).

Throughout the development of HFACS, several studies to assess reliability were performed using U.S. Navy/Marine Corps and U.S. Air Force aviation accident data. In each of these studies, three independent raters classified a number of causal factors and inter-rater reliabilities were calculated for each pair of raters using Cohen's kappa. Using an earlier version of HFACS, Walker (1996) and Rabbe (1996) examined inter-rater reliability using 93 U.S. Navy/Marine Corps controlled flight into terrain (CFIT) accidents (508 causal factors) and 79 F-16 accidents (190 causal factors) respectively. The overall reliabilities for each pair of raters are presented in Table 5. While the reliabilities were generally 'good', a detailed analysis revealed that reliabilities were best for variables within the preconditions level of the taxonomy, with slightly lower reliabilities within the unsafe acts and unsafe supervision tiers, respectively. Therefore, modifications were made to the taxonomy within these levels by adding categories and refining category definitions. Two additional studies were then conducted to assess the effects that these changes had on inter-rater reliabilities. These studies used the revised taxonomy to examine 733 human causal factors from 132 navy TACAIR and Rotary Wing accidents (Ranger, 1997) and 127 human causal factors from 41 B-1, B52, F-111, and F-4 accidents (Plourde, 1997). Results from these studies revealed increases in agreement levels across pairs of raters (Table 5). Again, additional modifications were made to the framework and a fifth study using what is now known as HFACS was conducted using 186 human causal factors from 77 A-10 accidents (Johnson, 1997). Overall, pair-wise reliabilities were found be 'excellent' by conventional standards in this study (see Table 5) and consistent across levels.

Table 5   Reliability of successive iterations of the HFACS framework

Author	Cohen's Kappa		
	Rater 1 vs Rater 2	Rater 1 vs Rater 3	Rater 2 vs Rater 3
Walker (1996)	.70	.60	.65
Rabbe (1996)	.69	.78	.62
Ranger (1997)	.81	.69	.80
Plourde (1997)	.89	.85	.86
Johnson (1997)	.93	.95	.95

Since these initial studies, a concerted effort has been made to ensure that the results of the analyses obtained via the application of HFACS and its predecessor taxonomies would be reliable and consistent across investigators. Furthermore, reliability analyses have been continually performed as the framework has been expanded to capture additional human factors issues or applied to other types of aviation accidents, such as commercial and general aviation accidents (Shappell and Wiegmann, 1999).

Usability

Usability refers to the practicality of a taxonomy, or the ease at which it can be turned into a practical methodology or made operational (Hollnagel, 1998). Put simply, the degree of acceptance of an approach is reflected by how easy the framework is to use and how often it is employed. Over the past five years, numerous Flight Surgeons, Aviation Safety Officers and other safety personnel within the U.S. Navy/Marine Corps and U.S. Army have been trained to reliably use HFACS after relatively few hours of instruction. Hundreds of other non-military professionals have also been trained to use the framework through full- and half-day workshops offered at a variety of government and professional society meetings.

Since its inception, the acceptability of HFACS and its predecessor frameworks has been repeatedly assessed and improved, based on inputs from those attending these training sessions, as well as feedback from operators in the field. Some changes that have improved acceptability included the rephrasing of technical or psychological terminology (e.g., slips, lapses and mistakes), to create terms that aviators would better understand (e.g. skill-based and decision errors). Another improvement simply required changing the name of the framework from the

Taxonomy of Unsafe Operations to Human Factors Analysis and Classification System or HFACS, to make the system more palatable to management. Perhaps the clearest evidence of the framework's usability however, is that large organisations like the U.S. Navy/Marine Corps and the U.S. Army have adopted HFACS as an accident investigation and data analysis tool. In addition, HFACS is currently being utilised within other organisations such as the FAA and NASA as a supplement to pre-existing systems (Ford, Jack, Crisp, and Sandusky, 1999).

Validity

The concept of validity concerns *what* a taxonomy captures or measures, and *how well* it does so (Anastasi, 1982). While there are multiple types of validity, three types (content, face, and construct validity) will be addressed here. Theoretically, the upper boundaries of these forms of validity are determined by the extent to which the framework meets the preceding four criterion (comprehensiveness, diagnosticity, reliability, and usability). For instance, assessing the content validity of a framework involves the systematic examination of the taxonomy to determine whether it covers a representative sample of the error domain to be measured. Face validity, on the other hand, refers to whether a taxonomy 'looks valid' to investigators who will use it or administrative personnel who decide on its use. Hence, content validity is directly related to comprehensiveness and reliably, whereas face validity is directly related to the acceptability of a framework, all of which have been shown to be relatively high for HFACS or its earlier versions.

The construct validity of an error taxonomy is somewhat more difficult to assess. Construct validity refers to the extent to which the framework taps into the underlying causes of errors and accidents. In this regard, construct validity is directly related to diagnosticity, or the ability of a framework to penetrate all levels of the system and reveal the underlying causes of errors and accidents. Another method for assessing construct validity, however, is through convergent and discriminant validation procedures (Anastasi, 1982). These procedures attempt to show that a framework identifies errors that are highly correlated with other variables in which they should theoretically be correlated (convergent validity) but do not correlate significantly with variables from which they should differ (discriminant validity). For example, it is commonly believed that controlled flight into terrain (CFIT) accidents are more often caused by a lack of visual reference (as would be the case when flying in bad weather or at night) than non-CFIT accidents. Given that this belief is true, an analysis using HFACS should differentiate between CFIT and non-CFIT accidents on at least two causal categories: adverse mental states (e.g., loss of situational awareness) and adverse physiological states (e.g., spatial disorientation).

Using an earlier version of the HFACS taxonomy, Shappell and Wiegmann (1997b) analysed causal factors associated with U.S. Navy/Marine Corps CFIT and non-CFIT accidents. Results of a series of logistic regressions and Chi Square analyses supported the hypothesised error correlations and differences between accident types. As expected, these analyses revealed that a larger proportion of CFIT accidents were associated with adverse mental and physiological states, as well as supervisory violations and personal readiness failures than were non-CFIT accidents. Thus, the application of the taxonomy produced an error profile consistent with the underlying theoretical causes of CFIT accidents distinct from non-CFIT accidents, further supporting the construct validity of the framework.

Summary and conclusion

The HFACS framework presented here bridges the gap between theory and practice by providing investigators with a comprehensive, user-friendly tool for identifying and classifying the human causes of aviation accidents. The framework, which is based upon Reason's (1990) model of latent and active failures, encompasses the multiple aspects of human error, including the conditions of operators and organisational failure. Consequently, the systematic application of the HFACS framework has resulted in the improved quality and quantity of information gathered during aviation accident investigations. Applications of the framework to database analysis have also begun to highlight critical human factors in need of further safety research. In addition, the HFACS framework has proven to be an effective instrument for monitoring the success or failure of specific intervention programmes designed to reduce specific types of human error and subsequent aviation accidents. In so doing, safety professionals have been able to readjust or reinforce intervention programmes to meet the changing needs of aviation safety. In summary, the development HFACS has proven to be a valuable first step in the establishment of a larger military and civil aviation safety programme whose ultimate goal is to reduce aviation accidents through systematic, data-driven investment strategies and the objective evaluation of intervention programmes.

References

Anastasi, A. (1988). *Psychological Testing (6th ed.)*. New York: Macmillan Publishing Co.
Bird, F. (1974). *Management guide to loss control.* Atlanta, GA: Institute Press.
Ford, C. N., Jack, T. D., Crisp, V. and Sandusky, R. (1999). Aviation accident causal analysis. *Advances in Aviation Safety Conference Proceedings* (P-343). Warrendale, PA: Society of Automotive Engineers Inc.
Heinrich, H. W., Petersen, D. and Roos, N. (1980). *Industrial accident prevention: A safety management approach (5th ed.).* New York: McGraw-Hill.

Helmreich, R. L. and Foushee, H. C. (1993). Why crew resource management? Empirical and theoretical bases of human factors training in aviation. In, E. L. Wiener, B. G. Kanki, and R. L. Helmreich (Eds.) *Cockpit resource management* (pp. 3-45). San Diego, CA: Academic Press.

Hollnagel, E. (1998). *Cognitive reliability and error analysis method (CREAM).* Oxford: Alden Group.

Johnson, W. (1997). *Classifying pilot human factor causes in A-10 Class A mishaps.* Unpublished graduate research project, Embry-Riddle Aeronautical University, Daytona Beach, Florida.

Jones, A.P. (1988). Climate and measurement of consensus: A discussion of 'organizational climate.' In, S.G. Cole, R.G. Demaree and W. Curtis (Eds.), *Applications of Interactionist Psychology: Essays in Honor of Saul B. Sells* (pp. 283-290). Hillsdale, NJ: Earlbaum.

Muchinsky, P.M. (1997). *Psychology applied to work (5th ed.).* Pacific Grove, CA: Brooks/Cole Publishing Co.

Murray, S. R. (1997). Deliberate decision making by aircraft pilots: A simple reminder to avoid decision making under panic. *The International Journal of Aviation Psychology, 7,* 83-100.

National Transportation Safety Board. (1973). *Eastern Air Lines, Inc., L-1011, N310EA, Miami, Florida, December 29, 1972.* (Tech. Report NTSB-AAR-73-14). Washington: National Transportation Safety Board.

National Transportation Safety Board. (1982). *Air Florida, Inc., Boeing 737-222, N62AF, Collision with 14th Street bridge, near Washington National Airport, Washington, D.C., January 13, 1982* (Tech. Report NTSB-AAR-82-8). Washington: National Transportation Safety Board.

Neubauer, J. Murdock, E., Fraser, J., and Veronneau, S. (1999). The year in review: Aviation safety update for FY 1998. *Aviation, Space and Environmental Medicine, 70,* 393-394.

O'Connor, S.L. and Hardiman, T. (1996). Human error in civil aircraft maintenance and dispatch: The basis of an error taxonomy. In, D. Harris (Ed) *Engineering Psychology and Cognitive Ergonomics Volume One - Transport Systems,* (pp. 315-322). Ashgate: Aldershot.

Orasanu, J. M. (1993). Decision-making in the cockpit. In, E. L. Wiener, B. G. Kanki and R. L. Helmreich (Eds.) *Cockpit resource management* (pp. 137-172). San Diego, CA: Academic Press.

Plourde, G. (1997). *Human factor causes in fighter-bomber mishaps: A validation of the Taxonomy of Unsafe Operations.* Unpublished graduate research project, Embry-Riddle Aeronautical University, Daytona Beach, Florida.

Pounds, J., Scarborough, A. and Shappell, S. (2000). *A human factors analysis of Air Traffic Control operational errors.* Abstract accepted for presentation at the Aerospace Medical Association Annual meeting in Houston, TX.

Primavera, L., Allison, D. and Alfonso, V. (1996). Measurement of dependent variables. In: Franklin, R., Allison, D. and Gorman, B. (Eds.) *Design and Analysis of Single-Case Research,* (pp. 41-92). Mahwah, NJ: Lawrence Earlbaum Associates.

Rabbe, L. (1996). *Categorizing Air Force F-16 mishaps using the Taxonomy of Unsafe Operations.* Unpublished graduate research project, Embry-Riddle Aeronautical University, Daytona Beach, Florida.

Ranger, K. (1997). *Inter-rater Reliability of the Taxonomy of Unsafe Operations. Unpublished graduate research project,* Embry-Riddle Aeronautical University, Daytona Beach, Florida.

Rasmussen, J. (1982). Human errors: A taxonomy for describing human malfunction in industrial installations. *Journal of Occupational Accidents, 4,* 311-333.

Reason, J. (1990). *Human error.* New York: Cambridge University Press.

Reinhart, R. O. (1996). *Basic flight physiology (2nd ed.).* New York: McGraw-Hill.

Schmidt, J.K., Schmorrow, D. and Hardee, M. (1998). A preliminary human factors analysis of Naval Aviation maintenance related mishaps. *Proceedings of the 1998 Airframe/Engine Maintenance and Repair Conference (P329),* Long Beach, CA.

Senders, J. W. and Moray, N. P. (1991). *Human error: Cause, prediction and reduction.* Hillsdale, NJ: Earlbaum.

Shappell, S. and Wiegmann, D. (1995). Controlled flight into terrain: The utility of an information processing approach to mishap causal factors. *Proceedings of the Eighth Symposium for Aviation Psychology,* Ohio State University, 1300-1306.

Shappell, S. A. and Wiegmann, D.A. (1996). U. S. naval aviation mishaps 1977-92: Differences between single- and dual-piloted aircraft. *Aviation, Space and Environmental Medicine, 67,* 65-69.

Shappell, S.A. and Wiegmann D. A. (1997a). A human error approach to accident investigation: The taxonomy of unsafe operations. *The International Journal of Aviation Psychology, 7,* 269-291.

Shappell, S. A. and Wiegmann, D. A. (1997b). Why would an experienced aviator fly a perfectly good aircraft into the ground? In, *Proceedings of the Ninth International Symposium on Aviation Psychology* (pp. 26-32). Columbus, OH: The Ohio State University.

Shappell, S. and Wiegmann, D. (1997c). A reliability analysis of the Taxonomy of Unsafe Operations. *Aviation, Space and Environmental Medicine, 68,* 620.

Shappell, S. and Wiegmann, D. (April, 1998). *Failure analysis classification system: A human factors approach to accident investigation.* Paper presented at the Society of Automotive Engineers: Advances in Aviation Safety Conference and Exposition, Daytona Beach, FL.

Shappell, S. and Wiegmann, D. (1999). Human error in commercial and corporate aviation: An analysis of FAR Part 121 and 135 mishaps using HFACS. *Aviation, Space and Environmental Medicine, 70*, 407.

Shappell, S., Wiegmann, D., Fraser, J., Gregory, G., Kinsey, P. and Squier, H (1999). Beyond mishap rates: A human factors analysis of U.S. Navy/Marine Corps TACAIR and rotary wing mishaps using HFACS. *Aviation, Space and Environmental Medicine, 70*, 416-417.

Walker, S. (1996). *A human factors examination of U.S. Naval controlled flight into terrain 'CFIT' accidents.* Unpublished graduate research project, Embry-Riddle Aeronautical University, Daytona Beach, Florida.

Wiegmann, D. and Shappell, S. (1995). Human factors in U.S. naval aviation mishaps: An information processing approach. *Proceedings of the Eighth Symposium for Aviation Psychology,* Ohio State University.

Wiegmann, D. and Shappell, S. (1997). Human factors analysis of post-accident data: Applying theoretical taxonomies of human error. *The International Journal of Aviation Psychology, 7,* 67-81.

Wiegmann, D. and Shappell, S. (April, 1998). *Human factors accident investigation: A much needed, but seldom called upon, investigative science.* Paper presented at the Society of Automotive Engineers: Advances in Aviation Safety Conference and Exposition, Daytona Beach, FL.

Wiegmann, D. A. and Shappell, S. A. (1999). Human error and crew resource management failures in Naval aviation mishaps: A review of U.S. Naval Safety Center data, 1990-96. *Aviation, Space and Environmental Medicine, 70,* 1147-1151.

Quantity and quality of sleep during the record manned space flight of 438 days

Alex Gundel*, Jürgen Drescher* and Valeri V. Polyakov**
*DLR Institute of Aerospace Medicine, Cologne, Germany
**Institute for Biomedical Problems, Moscow, Russia

Abstract

Sleep recordings during a 438-day spaceflight are evaluated as to how impaired sleep may compromise safety. The interpretation of results is embedded within a 30-day study of three other astronauts. During the first 30 days sleep was reduced to an average of a little more than six hours with large variation between nights, whereas later during the mission the astronaut got one more hour of sleep. Impaired quality of sleep seems to be an individual problem that does not affect all astronauts. It is suggested that private sleeping quarters and properly scheduled rest times present a way to avoid sleep problems.

Introduction

Sleep of operators is generally discussed under the premise that inappropriate quantity and quality of sleep result in fatigue and sleepiness and may compromise safety and success of an operation. This applies also for astronauts operating a spacecraft or conducting a research program. A survey about sleep complaints on the Space Shuttle has shown that the incidence of sleep disturbances was remarkably high (Santy, Kapanka, Davis and Stewart, 1988). This observation is supported by personal communications with astronauts that have worked on the Mir station. In spite of early observations of sleep disturbances and of a shortened sleep (Adey, Kado and Walter, 1967; Frost, Shumate, Booher and DeLucchi 1975; Litsov and Bulyko, 1983; Litsov and Shevchenko, 1985; Quadens and Green, 1984; Stoilova, Ponomariova, Myasnikov, Ivancheva, Polyakov, Zhukova and

Correspondence: Alexander Gundel, DLR Institute of Aerospace Medicine, Linder Höhe, D-51147 Cologne, Germany or alexander.gundel@dlr.de

Peneva, 1990; Polyakov, Posokhov, Ponomaryova, Zhukova, Kovrov and Vein 1994), consistent alterations in sleep parameters have been reported only recently in four astronauts onboard Mir (Gundel, Nalishiti, Reucher, Vejvoda and Zulley 1993; Gundel, Polyakov and Zulley; 1997) and in four astronauts on the Space Shuttle (Monk, Buysse, Billy, Kennedy and Willrich, 1998). Sleep disturbances in space may have a variety of causes. In individual astronauts they may be caused by exogenous factors like space motion sickness, perception of light flashes when high-energy protons hit the retina, emotional stress, high workload, an abnormal work schedule, thermal discomfort, noise, muscle pain, or an unsuitable sleeping bag. But also changes in the physiological basis for the regulation of sleep and the circadian clock may result in sleep disturbances.

The recuperative value of sleep is generally expressed by its duration and its continuity. Duration is measured by the total sleep time (TST) whereas continuity is often assessed by the quotient of TST and total time in bed (TIB). TIB is comprised of the time awake in bed and the time asleep (TST). The quotient TST/TIB has been named sleep efficiency.

A period of sleep is made up by several sleep cycles that last about 90 minutes. During a typical cycle, nonREM sleep gets deeper from stage two sleep to slow-wave sleep (stages three and four), which is then followed by REM sleep. The more tired someone is at the beginning of a sleep period the deeper is the sleep. The depth of sleep may be quantified by measuring the quantity of slow waves. REM sleep is regulated by the circadian clock and longer REM periods are observed around the circadian trough of body temperature in the early morning. The circadian clock is mainly synchronised by light to the 24-hour day. Since the light level in a spacecraft is low it may not be sufficient to synchronise the circadian rhythm, which then will run independently of the 24-hour day with a period that is longer than 24 hours.

However, the experiments of Monk et al. (1998) and Gundel et al. (1993, 1997) coincided in the conclusion that they did not observe a circadian free-run in space. Monk et al. (1998) did not find a consistent phase shift between ground measurements and recordings in space whereas Gundel et al. (1997) found a stable phase delay of about two hours in space.

The alterations of sleep parameters that were found in space concern the amount of slow-wave sleep and the cycles of nonREM and REM sleep, all being parameters for the physiological regulation of sleep. Monk et al. (1998) found a reduction of slow-wave sleep on the Space Shuttle whereas Gundel et al. (1993, 1997) report a shift of slow-wave sleep from the first sleep cycle to the second cycle but no overall reduction of slow-wave sleep on the Mir space station. In addition, the first nonREM period, i.e. the latency to the first occurrence of REM sleep, was shortened.

Based on the findings in four astronauts who lived on board the Mir station for up to one month (Gundel et al. 1997), data obtained in a single astronaut who stayed in space for 438 days are evaluated to address the following questions:

- How do sleep structure and circadian rhythms develop during a prolonged stay in space?
- Do the sleep recordings during a long-term mission give a clue for an explanation why sleep is shorter and in some astronauts more disturbed?
- Do sleeping conditions in space compromise safety?

Method

At the beginning of his record flight the astronaut was 52 years of age. The other three astronauts were 39, 47, and 53 years old at the time of their mission. All astronauts who served the experiments as subjects gave their informed consent to this study that complied with the recommendations of the Declaration of Helsinki.

Astronauts spent the first two days and nights of their space flight in the launch vehicle Soyuz before they entered the orbital complex Mir. The slow approach of Soyuz to the Mir station is common to all missions. The experiments could begin only after the astronauts arrived on Mir. During the record flight sleep polygraphies were obtained in three phases of about 1-month duration each. The first phase comprised the flight days 3 to 30 (polysomnographies in nights 3, 4, 16, 17, 23, 29 and 30), the second measurement period occurred between days 183 and 215 (nights 183, 184, 191, 192, 196, 197, 205, 206, 213 and 215) and the last phase lasted from day 395 until day 425 (nights 395, 396, 403, 405, 410, 411, 416, 417, 424 and 425). All but two polysomnographies of the other three subjects were obtained between day 3 and day 30 in space. For the record flight 48-hour experimental measurement blocks that were a week apart were planned and requested. The recordings that were actually obtained reflect the operational constraints for the experiments on board Mir.

For a comparison of data that were obtained during the mission, baseline measurements were taken for up to six days, including a night for adaptation to the recording procedures. Baseline experiments were conducted prior to the mission at least four weeks before launch. Immediately before launch astronauts were occupied by operational work and their availability for scientific experiments was limited.

Mir space flights were operated under the local time of the ground control and astronaut training center, i.e. working and sleeping were scheduled accordingly. When subjects spent the days prior to mission close to the launch site which is two time zones eastward of the training site, they were forced to keep their sleeping times and their meals according to the local time of mission control, too. Thus there was no shift in time between baseline, pre-mission period and the mission. The training programme for the astronauts continued during baseline measurements. They lived in their apartments and left during the day to attend classes and for other activities. Astronauts did not exercise during baseline measurements but sometimes exercised during mission measurement blocks. As on the orbital complex where also operational constraints determined sleeping times to some extent, subjects were free to choose their sleeping times as during baseline. They were encouraged to stick to their habitual sleeping times.

As a control for possible masking effects imposed by the rest-activity cycle bedtimes during baseline and mission measurements were compared. Astronauts went to bed on the average 1:01 hours later during the first 30 mission days than during baseline days (00:19 and 01:20 hours, respectively). This difference was not statistically significant (repeated measure ANOVA $F_{1,3}=1.05$, p=0.38). The mean get-up time was delayed by 50 minutes during the first 30 days in space.

The environmental temperature could not be controlled during any period of the experiments. Information about the actual exposure to light during the mission could not be obtained. In general, astronauts are exposed only to artificial light in the Mir station. However, under circumstances when they look out of a window they may receive sunlight depending on the position of the Mir station.

The main hardware item used was an Oxford Medilog 8-channel recorder that allows the continuous recording of body temperature for 24 hours in addition to sleep polygraphies. Equipment had to be suitable to be handled only by the astronauts themselves without assistance from others. To meet these constraints, an elastic head-band with integrated Ag/AgCl-electrodes was used for polygraphic recordings. EEG electrodes were placed according to the international 10-20 system. The electrode positions of this band were C3, C4, Cz (ground electrode), and O2. Two EOG signals were derived from the forehead. The band provided also clip-on connectors for 4 disposable electrodes that served as mastoid references (A1, A2) and as EMG derivations from the neck. Thus the seven polygraphic channels were C4-A1, C3-A2, O2-A1, EOG1-A2, EOG2-A1, EMG1-A2, and EMG2-A1. This setting provided some useful redundancy. Body temperature was measured by a rectal thermistor probe.

In addition to the recordings, a general sleep questionnaire was filled out by the astronauts after each sleep recording. However, it turned out that cultural differences between astronauts resulted in different attitudes towards the sleep questionnaire. Therefore, these questionnaires were used only as a means to help analysing the tape recordings. Results from the sleep questionnaire will not be presented.

Tapes with the recorded polysomnographies were brought back to earth and sent to our laboratory in Cologne for evaluation. In a first step, data were converted from analogue to digital. The computer allowed a visual scoring of sleep stages in 30-s epochs according to Rechtschaffen and Kales (1968). At the same time signal quality was screened and rated for artefacts and completeness. The artefact rating served as input for subsequent automatic analysis. This included evaluation of the time course of body temperature and of EEG power density. EEG power density during sleep is dominated by slow-wave activity. To assess amplitudes of delta waves broadband power was determined in the frequency range from 0.5 to 5.0 Hz. Power density was calculated for the channels C3 and C4 and then averaged. Epochs with artefacts were excluded from the power analysis resulting in missing values. These missing values were linearly interpolated. The amount of missing values was small and could not influence results substantially. Circadian phase was determined from the minimum in body temperature after non-parametric regression (Gasser, Müller, and Mammitzsch 1985) of values that were obtained every 30 seconds. Non-parametric regression analysis resulted in a smoothing of temperature curves. A second phase estimate was obtained by a Fourier transformation using a basic period of 24 hours and three higher harmonics. Statistical evaluation of data was conducted by a repeated measure ANOVA using SAS software.

Results

Circadian phases were estimated using body temperature curves of individual days. The estimation procedures that were applied, i.e. non-parametric local smoothing (Gasser et al. 1985) and Fourier transformation, yielded similar times for the absolute daily minimum in body temperature. During the first 30 days of the record mission the average phase delay (n=6 nights) was 2:52±2:55 hours when the phases were estimated by a Fourier transformation and 3:08±2:21 hours when the estimates were obtained by local smoothing. For the second experimental period (mission days 183-215) these values (n=10) were 3:25±1:16 and 4:05±1:36 hours, respectively, and for the third period (mission days 395-425) a phase delay of 1:34±3:59 hours (1:34±3:39) hours was observed (n=8). Indications for a circadian free-run were not found.

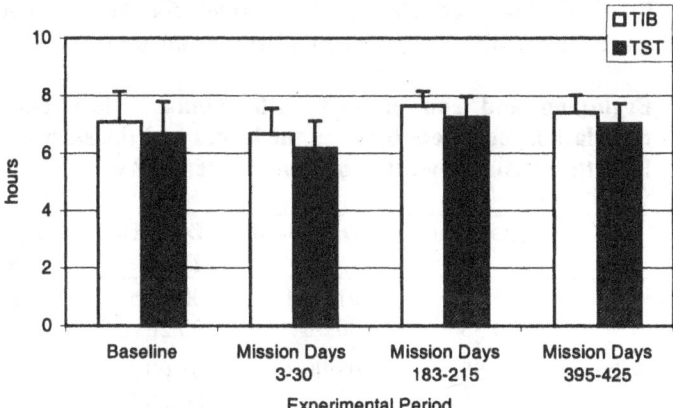

Figure 1 Mean time in bed (TIB) and mean total sleep time (TST) during baseline nights (n=6) and three experimental periods (n=7, 10, 8) during the record mission of 438 days are displayed together with standard deviations

For the four astronauts including the record astronaut individual averages of the phase estimates were statistically analysed for the first 30 days by a repeated measure ANOVA with repetitions (mission and baseline) on one factor. These averages result in a mean phase delay of 2:01 hours (Fourier analysis) or 2:23 hours (local smoothing). The delay was significant for the estimate obtained by Fourier analysis ($F_{1,3}$=15.30, p=0.03) and showed a trend ($F_{1,3}$=7.82, p=0.07) for the other estimate.

The quantity of sleep is measured as total sleep time (TST) during time in bed (TIB). It is displayed in figure 1. TIB is shortest during the first 30 days in space (6:40±0:54 hours) and longer later during mission amounting to 7:39±0:30 hours for the second and 7:25±0:37 hours for the third measurement period. The lengthening of TIB from the first experimental period to the second and the third one was statistically significant (t-test, p<0.05). Accordingly, the average TST is shortest in the beginning of the record flight (6:11±0:58 hours) and longer in the course of the mission with 7:15±0:45 and 7:02±0:43 hours. Both differences to the first experimental period are significant (t-test, p<0.05). The standard deviation of TIB was larger during baseline and the first mission period (1:04 and 0:54 hours) than later during mission (0:30 and 0:37 hours).

A close inspection of sleep timing shows that there was a relation between TIB and actual bedtimes. The astronaut got up at 6:50±0:45 hours (mean, n=6) during baseline and at around 8:00 hours throughout the mission (table 1). Getting up times were more regular during mission (compare table 1). The bedtimes were with 23:44±0:55, 01:20±0:56, 0:21±0:26, and 0:39±0:32 hours more variable than the end of sleep. The differences in the standard deviation corresponded with those of TIB (figure 1). A correlation analysis (rank correlations) revealed that the later the astronaut went to bed the shorter TIB was (table 1).

Table 1 Beginning and end of TIB with standard deviation and the correlation coefficient between the length and the start of TIB. The later the astronaut went to bed the shorter TIB was

	Baseline	Days 3-30	Days 183-215	Days 395-425
Start of TIB (hours)	23:44 ± 00:55	01:20 ± 00:56	00:21 ± 00:26	00:39 ± 00:32
End of TIB (hours)	06:50 ± 00:45	08:00 ± 00:19	08:00 ± 00:20	08:06 ± 00:24
Correlation between the length and the start of TIB	-0.52 (n.s.)	-0.96 (p<0.05)	-0.67 (p<0.05)	-0.75 (p<0.05)

Sleep quality was evaluated according to Rechtschaffen and Kales, and table 2 presents results for sleep efficiency (TST divided by TIB) and sleep latency, i.e. latency to the first stage two sleep. Both parameters did not show a significant variation neither in the course of the mission nor compared to baseline.

Table 2 Sleep efficiency (TST divided by TIB) and sleep latency, i.e. the latency to the first stage 2 sleep, for baseline and three periods during the spaceflight

	Baseline	Days 3-30	Days 183-215	Days 395-425
Sleep efficiency	0.94 ± 0.06	0.92 ± 0.05	0.95 ± 0.04	0.95 ± 0.04
Sleep latency (min)	5.2 ± 2.9	6.6 ± 4.7	11.6 ± 12.9	5.2 ± 3.4

Figure 2 displays sleep architecture up to the third non-REM period. Sleep was terminated during the third REM sleep period in some of the nights. Therefore, the third REM phase and later sleep were excluded from the analysis of sleep structure. Non-REM phases included also stage one sleep. Comparing initial mission and baseline data figure 2 shows that the latency to the first REM sleep period was shorter in space. The second non-REM period showed more delta sleep in space than on ground. The redistribution of slow-wave sleep to later cycles seems to continue also in the second and third experimental period, where the latency to REM sleep is not shortened any more. These qualitatively described changes are not statistically significant for the record astronaut.

Data obtained from the four astronauts during baseline and the first 30 days in space were analysed by a repeated measure ANOVA with the factors 'mission' and 'sleep cycle'. Analysis of the duration of the first three non-REM periods resulted in a significant interaction of 'mission' and 'sleep cycle' ($F_{2,6}=8.16$, $p=0.020$). Contrasts to the average of the other two sleep cycles revealed that the significant interaction was caused by the first non-REM period ($F_{1,3}=15.09$, $p=0.030$), i.e. the shorter REM latency in space (56.2 min versus 71.3 min on ground). The third non-REM period showed a trend ($F_{1,3}=9.12$, $p=0.057$) to being longer in space (80.4 min versus 67.9 min on the ground).

The amount of slow-wave sleep during a non-REM phase was quantified as the product of the average delta power and the duration of that particular non-REM period. ANOVAs were conducted with logarithmically transformed values. The ANOVA for the amount of slow-wave sleep showed a trend ($F_{2,6}=4.56$, $p=0.071$) for the interaction of the factors 'mission' and 'sleep cycle'. The contrasts showed that the higher amount of slow-wave sleep in the second non-REM period on board Mir is responsible for this statistical effect ($F_{1,3}=28.87$, $p=0.013$). Both main effects were not significant.

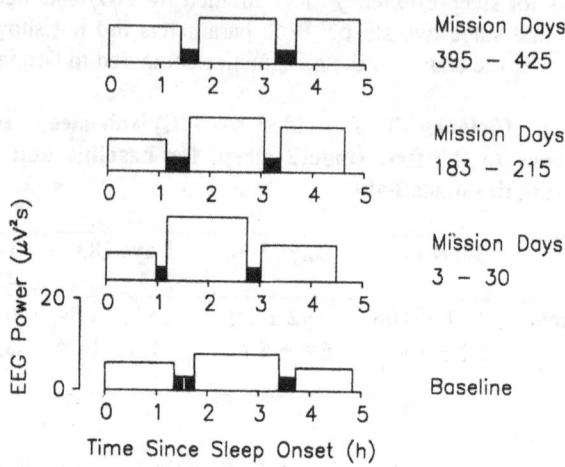

Figure 2 Average sleep structure for baseline sleep and sleep during three experimental periods during the record mission. The height (y-axis) of an open non-REM area corresponds to the average power of slow waves in that particular non-REM period. The height of hatched REM areas has been arbitrarily chosen for display

Discussion

Sleep quantity data that were obtained during a 438-day space mission suggest a simple interpretation for the reduced amount of sleep frequently reported, e.g. for a 17-day mission (Monk et al. 1998) and for missions up to 30 days (Gundel et al., 1997). During the first 30 days of the record mission the astronaut slept on average half an hour (6.17 hours) less than on the ground before the mission (6.67 hours). The total sleep time of 6.17 hours is very close to values reported by Gundel et al. (1997) and by Monk et al. (1998) who observed averages of 6.11 and 6.04 hours, respectively. Later during the record mission total sleep time was increased by an hour to more than seven hours.

Total sleep time was correlated to the time when the astronaut went to bed. The later the astronaut began to sleep the shorter his sleep was. The wake-up times were largely determined by the next day's schedule whereas the bedtime was usually chosen according to work that had to be finished and to the social life on board Mir. Workload that is caused, by e.g. repair work, and the need to communicate is particularly high at the beginning of a stay in space leading to a large variation in bedtimes and to a delay of bedtimes. During later periods of the mission when routine work became more prominent, bedtimes were not as variable and commenced more than an hour earlier. This simple explanation of reduced sleep times in space probably holds also for other observations of reduced sleep in space. It seems unlikely now that microgravity changes sleeping times directly or indirectly.

Human beings are able to adapt to restricted sleeping hours to some extent and will get as much slow-wave sleep during restricted as during normal sleeping periods (Brunner, Dijk, and Borbély, 1993). A chronic restriction to six hours is reported to have no effect on subjective fatigue and psychomotor performance during the day (Horne and Wilkinson, 1985) or perhaps a small effect (Rosenthal, Roehrs, Rosen, and Roth, 1993) only. However, a reduction of sleep to about five hours is followed by impaired subjective fatigue and sleepiness already after the first night. Some aspects of psychomotor vigilance performance react only after the second night of five hours sleep (Dinges, Pack, Williams, Gillen, Powell, Ott, Aptowicz and Pack, 1997).

The laboratory results about sleep restriction mean that a total sleep time of 6 hours does not lead to a performance reduction if the sleep duration is constant. Therefore, the variation in sleep duration is of concern since an average sleep time of six hours that has a standard deviation of about one hour means that there may be several nights with sleep of five hours or less. These nights are indeed followed by an increased daytime sleepiness and fatigue and by an impairment of psychomotor performance.

Several measures to avoid a sleep regime with partial sleep deprivation are possible. We would recommend establishing private sleeping quarters that ensure privacy during rest times and to schedule rest times for an entire mission properly.

This view is supported by the study of psychomotor performance during the 438-day space mission (Manzey, Lorenz and Poljakov, 1998) and by an analysis of work-rest schedules and crew errors in a larger astronaut population on the Mir station (Nechaev, Myasnikov, Stepanova, Kozerenko, Isaev, and Bronnikov, 1998; Nechaev, 1999). The study of psychomotor performance showed impaired tracking performance and time-sharing as well as an impaired mood during the first three weeks in space whereas these measures were stable later during the mission. The analysis of work-rest schedules (Nechaev et al., 1998; Nechaev, 1999) found that the 'tensity' of the work-rest schedule was found positively correlated to crew errors. The tensity of a work-rest schedule was defined as a complex metric that describes disturbances forced on the sleep-wake cycle by e.g. onboard alarms during night and by night work of more than three hours (Nechaev et al., 1998; Nechaev, 1999).

Though there are many reasons for a reduced sleep quality during a space mission, data suggest that bad sleep is an individual problem (Gundel et al., 1997). Three out of four astronauts that were studied did not show a marked reduction of sleep quality during their mission. Only one astronaut complained about serious insomnia of unknown origin. In particular, the record mission did not show a deterioration of sleep quality in the course of the mission. The record astronaut who did not experience bad sleep in space took several countermeasures. He slept in the Kristal module of the Mir station well separated from the command module. He chose a place to fasten his sleeping bag that provided best thermal comfort and he tried to shield his place from radiation by a stack of old batteries. In addition, he found tactile stimuli provided by the pillow important. In choosing the countermeasures he benefited from his experiences from an earlier mission when he reported worse sleep than during the record mission.

It may be concluded that micro-gravity per se does not have an important impact on sleep quality and quantity and that observed changes are due to the living and working conditions in a spacecraft. However, sleep regulation i.e. the structure of sleep may be altered by microgravity indirectly (Gundel et al., 1997). The observed alterations in sleep regulation do not present a transient phenomenon but persisted throughout the experiments. These changes seem to continue during the length of the record mission with a tendency to delay the occurrence of slow-wave sleep even more.

Circadian phase as assessed by the trough in core body temperature is delayed in astronauts during spaceflight. The delay relative to ground-based measurements amounts to about two hours. The phase delay appeared already on the first day when measurements were possible, i.e. after leaving the launch vehicle and entering the Mir station about two days after launch. A circadian free-run was not observed in the entire course of the record mission. A free-run should occur if bright light would have been the only effective circadian zeitgeber (Wever, Polasek, and Wildgruber 1983, Czeisler, Kronauer, Allan, Duffy, Jewett, Brown, and Ronda, 1989) since there is no natural 24-hour light-dark cycle in an orbiting spacecraft. However, recent studies showed that also light of lower intensity may synchronize the circadian system to a 24-hour day (Boivin, Duffy, Kronauer and Czeisler, 1996). Also non-photic or social time cues or the combination of photic and non-photic zeitgebers may possibly synchronise body clock and 24-hour day (Wever, 1979).

In conclusion, the circadian system does not free-run but shows a phase delay in astronauts. This phase delay is likely the result of changes in zeitgeber strength and zeitgeber structure aboard Mir. A shortened REM latency and more slow-wave sleep in the second non-REM period characterise the change in sleep structure that is a con-sequence of microgravity. Both phenomena, the circadian phase delay and the alteration of sleep structure, present a persistent adaptation to the space environment. Sleep disturbances occur in individual astronauts. The observed sleep disturbances seem neither to result from the circadian phase delay nor from the alteration of sleep structure. However, a shorter duration of sleep was observed initially during missions. The shortened sleep included sleep periods of clearly less than 6 hours leading to an acute sleep deprivation that has the potential to compromise safety of operations. To avoid shortened sleep privacy of astronauts should be ensured and times for rest allocated properly.

References

Adey, W.A., Kado, R.T. and Walter, D.O. (1967). Computer analysis of EEG data from Gemini flight GT-7. *Aerospace Medicine, 38,* 345-359.

Boivin, D.B., Duffy, J.F., Kronauer R.E. and Czeisler, C.A. (1996). Dose-response relationships for resetting of human circadian clock by light. *Nature, 379,* 540-542.

Brunner, D.P., Dijk, D.-J. and Borbély, A.A. (1993). Repeated partial sleep deprivation progressively changes the EEG during sleep and wakefulness. *Sleep, 16,* 100-113.

Czeisler, C.A., Kronauer, R.E., Allan, J.S., Duffy, J.F., Jewett, M.E., Brown, E.N. and Ronda, J.M. (1989). Bright light induction of strong (type 0) resetting of the human circadian pacemaker. *Science, 244,* 1328-1333.

Dinges, D.F., Pack, F., Williams, K., Gillen, K.A., Powell, J.W., Ott, G.E., Aptowicz and Pack, A.I. (1997). Cumulative Sleepiness, mood disturbance, and psychomotor vigilance performance decrements during a week of sleep restricted to 4-5 hours per night. *Sleep, 20,* 267-277.

Frost, J.D., Shumate, W.H., Booher, C.R. and DeLucchi, M.R. (1975). The Skylab sleep monitoring experiment: methodology and initial results. *Acta Astronautica, 2,* 319-336.

Gasser, T., Müller, H.G. and Mammitzsch, V. (1985). Kernels for nonparametric curve estimation. *Journal of the Royal Statistical Society B, 47,* 238-252.

Gundel, A., Nalishiti, V., Reucher, E., Vejvoda, M. and Zulley, J. (1993). Sleep and circadian rhythm during a short space mission. *Clinical Investigator, 71,* 718-724.

Gundel, A., Polyakov, V.V. and Zulley, J. (1997). The alteration of human sleep and circadian rhythms during spaceflight. *Journal of Sleep Research, 6,* 1-8.

Horne, J.A. and Wilkinson, S. (1985). Chronic sleep reduction: Daytime vigilance performance and EEG measures of sleepiness with particular reference to 'practice' effects. *Psychophysiology, 22,* 69-78.

Litsov, A.N. and Bulyko, V.I. (1983). Principles of organization of rational schedules for crew work and rest during a long-term spaceflight. *USSR Report-Space Biology and Aerospace Medicine, 17,* 9-13.

Litsov, A.N. and Shevchenko, V.F. (1985). Psychophysiological distinctions of organization and regulation of daily cyclograms of crew activities during long-term space-flight. *USSR Report-Space Biology and Aerospace Medicine, 19,* 12-18.

Manzey, D., Lorenz, B. and Poljakov, V. (1998). Mental performance in extreme environments: results from a performance monitoring study during a 438-day spaceflight. *Ergonomics, 41,* 537-559.

Monk, T.H., Buysse, D.J., Billy, B.D., Kennedy, K.S. and Willrich, L.M. (1998). Sleep and circadian rhythms in four orbiting astronauts. *Journal of Biological Rhythms, 13,* 188-201.

Nechaev, A.P., Myasnikov, V.I., Stepanova, S.I., Kozerenko, O.P., Isaev, G.F. and Bronnikov, S.V. (1998). Methodological approach to study of cosmonauts errors and its instrumental support. *Acta Astronautica, 42*, 331-338.

Nechaev, A.P. (1999). Interelationship of erroneous actions of cosmonauts, their psychophysiological state, and work-rest schedule peculiarities. *Aviakosmicheskaya i Ecologicheskaya Meditsina, 33*, 9-12.

Polyakov, V.V., Posokhov, S.I., Ponomaryova, I.P., Zhukova, O.P., Kovrov, G.V. and Vein, A.M. (1994). Sleep in space flight. *Aerospace and Environmental Medicine, 28*, 4-7.

Quadens, O. and Green, H. (1984). Eye movements during sleep in weightlessness. *Science, 245*, 221-222.

Rechtschaffen, A. and Kales, A. (1968). *A manual of standardized terminology, techniques and scoring system for sleep stages of human subjects.* UCLA BIS/BRI, Los Angeles.

Rosenthal, L., Roehrs, T.A., Rosen, A. and Roth, T. (1993). Level of sleepiness and total sleep time following various time in bed conditions. *Sleep, 16*, 226-232.

Santy, P.A., Kapanka, H., Davis, J.R. and Stewart, D.F. (1989). Analysis of sleep on Shuttle missions. *Aviation, Space and Environmental Medicine, 59*, 1094-1097.

Stoilova, I., Ponomariova, I.P., Myasnikov, V.I., Ivancheva, H., Polyakov, V.V., Zhukova, O.P. and Peneva, N. (1990). Study of sleep during a prolonged space flight of the 'Mir' orbiting station. In, K. Boda (Ed.) *Current trends in cosmic biology and medicine* (pp. 85-89). Slovak Academy of Sciences, Ivanka Pri Dunaji.

Wever, R.A. (1979). *The circadian system of man.* Springer, New York.

Wever, R.A., Polasek, J. and Wildgruber, C.M. (1983). Bright light affects human circadian rhythms. *Pflügers Archiv, 396*, 85-87.

CRITICAL INCIDENTS

Precautionary emergency evacuations: is it better to be safe *and* sorry?

Lauren Thomas
Cranfield University, UK

'When the engine started, flames shot out of the back of the engine, and a non revenue flight attendant seated in the aft cabin of the airplane saw the flames, and told the flight attendant on duty in the back of the airplane that the engine was on fire. The flight attendant on duty then opened both aft cabin doors and deployed both slides. Thirteen passengers then exited the airplane through the aft doors while the engines were running. The flight crew piloting the aircraft was unaware of the flight attendant initiated evacuation until they were told by the ground crew attending to the airplane.' (NTSB, 2000a)

'A Boeing 737... was inadvertently evacuated on the taxiway at New Tokyo International Airport... The evacuation was precipitated when a passenger saw flames coming out of the exhaust of the number one engine due to a hot start. This passenger then yelled "Fire!". A flight attendant then opened an emergency door, and 322 of the 362 passengers evacuated before the evacuation could be stopped. Three passengers received serious injuries and one passenger received a minor injury during the evacuation.' (NTSB, 1998)

The incidents above are taken directly from the National Transportation Safety Board Accident/Incident database. Although not totally representative, these extracts serve to highlight the fact that cabin crew can deploy emergency egress

Correspondence: Lauren Thomas, Human Factors Group, College of Aeronautics, Cranfield University, Cranfield, Bedford, MK43 0AL, United Kingdom, or l.thomas@cranfield.ac.uk.

systems, and evacuate passengers, without the flight crew being aware of the situation. It is also apparently possible to 'inadvertently' evacuate 322 passengers if one of them observes a hot start. Situations such as these have been termed 'precautionary emergency evacuations' (PEEvacs).

Precautionary emergency evacuations are those which occur when an emergency evacuation or unscheduled deplanement is initiated in the belief that there is an imminent threat to safety, and where it later transpires that this was not the case. These precautionary emergency evacuations may be initiated by flight crew or flight attendants, or, more rarely, passengers and ground crew. For such an event to occur, at least one person must perceive an imminent and significant risk to him or herself and/or others. To a certain extent then, one could argue that such incidents occur because it is better to be safe than sorry.

Recent research suggests that such evacuations and deplanements of this nature occur frequently. For example, Hynes (1999) searched the FAA AIDS system, the NTSB accident database, and the NASA Aviation Safety Reporting System for such events, and supplemented this data with information from surveys of airport managers. He found that between 1 January 1988 and 1 November 1996, 519 incidents of this nature had taken place. During this period, a precautionary emergency evacuation had taken place once every five or six days, involving around 4,759 people per year. On average, 101 people per year received injuries, the majority of which were sustained on emergency escape slides. The costs of personal injury alone were estimated at $8.54 million.

Evacuating an aircraft is not without risk. In a further study of 109 precautionary emergency evacuations between February 1994 and November 1996, Hynes (2000) found that 19 precautionary emergency evacuations had resulted in injuries to 190 passengers and three crewmembers, with 86% of those reporting injuries receiving medical assistance. Detailed information on the injuries sustained was available for only 135 evacuees. These included injuries to the back and neck, to the legs and feet, cuts and abrasions, abdominal pains and chest pains, sprains, and, in 11 cases, broken bones.

It is evidently safer to remain on board the aircraft if there is no imminent threat to safety. While a broken bone is a relatively positive outcome in an emergency situation, the injury is a liability if it is incurred where an evacuation was not required. Serious accidents are always investigated with a view to determining the causal factors, and reducing the probability of such events occurring again. PEEvacs too are becoming an acknowledged source of valuable safety information. For example, such evacuations were included in a recent NTSB safety study (NTSB 2000b). This research involved a detailed study of 46 evacuation cases, in which questionnaires were sent to all flight crew, flight attendants, passengers and aircraft rescue and firefighting units involved. Data from these 46 evacuations were used to make 20 new safety recommendations to the FAA, and to reiterate three previous ones.

However, the NTSB study was a special focus on evacuation safety, and was directly aimed at collecting the relevant data. There is no formal, standardised method for collecting data on PEEvacs per se. Information on such events is known to be difficult to obtain. For example, Hynes stressed that there was a lack of data available for his studies, and also cites three particular reasons why this might have been the case. Firstly, the personnel involved sought to avoid media coverage and other public disclosure of evacuation events. Secondly, some airport representatives denied that PEEvacs had taken place at their airports, suggesting either a reluctance to make this information available, or a lack of awareness about the event having taken place. Finally, 'litigation associated with emergency evacuations is almost always settled out of court, and frequently includes an agreement by all parties not to disclose publicly any information relating to the case' (1999, p. 5).

Until routine data are available to establish the causes of these events, action to reduce their frequency and the number of injuries associated with them is difficult. Since it is now evident that a large number of evacuations and injuries occur in situations which are not critical, measures to reduce the frequency of these events, and the injuries associated with them, are now overdue. Standardised information on the causes of these evacuations, including data relating to who initiated the evacuation, how, and the numbers and types of injuries sustained, is urgently required.

References

Hynes, M.K. (1999). *Frequency and Costs of Transport Airplane Precautionary Emergency Evacuations.* Washington, D.C.; DOT/FAA/AM-99/30.

Hynes, M.K. (2000). *Evacuee Injuries and Demographics in Transport Airplane Precautionary Emergency Evacuations.* Washington, D.C.; DOT/FAA/AM-00/11.

National Transportation Safety Board (1998). Extract from Accident/Incident Database, Factual Report Number DCA98WA043.

National Transportation Safety Board (2000a). Extract from Accident/Incident Database, Preliminary Report Number MIA00SA106.

National Transportation Safety Board (2000b). *Safety Study: Emergency Evacuation of Commercial Airplanes.* (Report # PB2000-917002). Washington, D.C.: NTSB.

Calendar of Events

March 5-8 2001 **Ohio State University, Columbus, Ohio, USA**
11th International Symposium in Aviation Psychology

Contact Dr. Richard Jensen, Department of Aerospace Engineering, Applied Mechanics and Aviation, Ohio State University, 164 West 19th Avenue, Columbus, OH 43210-1110, USA.
Fax: +1 614 292 1014
E-mail: rjensen@pop.service.ohio-state.edu

10-12 April 2001 **Royal Agricultural College, Cirencester, UK**
Ergonomics Society 2001 Conference

Contact Annual Conference Programme Secretary; The Ergonomics Society; Devonshire House; Devonshire Square; Loughborough; Leics. LE11 3DW, UK

18-21 June 2001 **University of Manchester Institute of Science and Technology (UMIST), Manchester, UK**
People in Control - An International Conference on Human Interfaces in Control Rooms, Cockpits and Command Centres

Contact Sarah Nash: E-mail: pic2001@iee.org.uk
Web site http://www.iee.org.uk/conf/PIC2001

5-10 August 2001 **New Orleans, Louisiana, USA**
HCI International 2001

Contact Kim Gilbert; School of Industrial Engineering; Purdue University; 1287 Grissom Hall; West Lafayette; IN 47907-1287, USA
Tel: +1 765 494 5426: Fax +1 765 494 0874
E-mail: kgilbert@ecn.purdue.edu
Web site http://hcii2001.engr.wisc.edu

Human Factors and Aerospace Safety
AN INTERNATIONAL JOURNAL
Volume 1, 2001, Quarterly, ISSN: 1468 9456

Subscription Order Form

UK/Europe/RoW: If you would like to subscribe to *Human Factors and Aerospace Safety*, please fill out the subscription form below and return it to: Nicky Staszkiewicz, Subscriptions Department, Ashgate Publishing Limited, Gower House, Croft Road, Aldershot, Hampshire, GU11 3HR, UK, Tel: +44 (0) 1252 351804, Fax: +44 (0) 1252 351859, E-mail: nstaszkiewicz@gowerpub.com
Subscription Rates: Institutions: £120.00 Individuals: £50.00 * + postage and packing
(*Postage & packing: UK/Europe: free of charge, RoW: £12.00)

North/South America: Please contact: Suzanne Sprague, Customer Service Manager, Ashgate Publishing, 2252 Ridge Road, Brookfield, VT 05036-9704, USA, Tel: 1-800-535-9544, Fax: 1-802-276-3837, E-mail: orders@ashgate.com
Subscription Rates: Institutions: $175.00 Individuals: $75.00 * + postage and packing
(*Postage & packing: North America: $5.95 (add $0.35 per additional copy)
South America: $15.00 (add $2.50 per additional copy))

❑ Please send me a sample copy of *Human Factors and Aerospace Safety*

❑ I wish to place an order for ____ annual subscription(s)
    to *Human Factors and Aerospace Safety*

❑ I enclose a cheque for £ _____ made payable to:
    Ashgate Publishing Limited Distribution Account (UK/Europe/RoW only)

❑ Please invoice me/my company/institution (delete as appropriate)

❑ Please charge my Visa/Mastercard/Access/American Express (delete as appropriate)

Account No. _____ Expiry Date _____

Signature _____
If your credit card address differs from the delivery address given below, please supply details on a separate sheet.

Name _____ Position _____

Company/Institution _____

Delivery Address _____

_____

_____

Postcode/Zipcode _____ Telephone _____

Customers outside the UK, please enter your VAT/IVA number here _____
Failure to do so could result in the considerable delay of your order.

Prices are subject to change without notice. If you do not wish to receive offers of goods from Ashgate or any other organization, please write to: Susanne Geerken, Ashgate Publishing Limited, Gower House, Croft Road, Aldershot, Hampshire, GU11 3HR, UK